THE
HIGH
PERFORMANCE
CUSTOMER INSIGHT
PROFESSIONAL

How to
make sense
of the evidence,
build the story and
turn insights into action

DVL SMITH

CONTENTS

ACKNOWLEDGEMENTS

I would like to thank Jo Smith for her judgement in making the critical decisions about what to include in the book and the level to which each topic should be taken in providing the reader with actionable substance.

Thanks also goes to Anne Scott for editing the text in such a skilled and professional way and for taking responsibility for the design and layout of the book.

I would like to thank Alexia Smith for her expertise and patience in helping to prepare the drafts of the book. This drafting process was vital in ensuring we were focusing on the right content in an engaging way.

AUTHOR

David VL Smith is the Founder and Director of DVL Smith, a leading UK insight consultancy. He is a Visiting Professor at the University of Hertfordshire Business School.

He is a former Vice President of ESOMAR and a former Chairman of the UK Market Research Society (MRS).

David holds a PhD in Organisational Psychology from the University of London. He is a Graduate Member of the British Psychological Society. He is a Fellow of the Market Research Society, a Fellow of the Chartered Institute of Marketing and also a Fellow of the Institute of Business Consultants.

He holds the MRS Silver Medal, the AURA Award for Driving the Insight Industry Forward, and ESOMAR's prestigious Excellence in Marketing Intelligence Award.

David is the author of *Inside Information - Making Sense of Marketing Data* and *The Art and Science of Interpreting Market Research Evidence*, both published by John Wiley.

PREFACE

I have spent several decades undertaking insight projects for a wide range of organisations across the world drawn from a variety of sectors on a host of business challenges. It is a career that I have found enjoyable and rewarding.

I have always been aware that providing insight-driven solutions requires a range of higher order technical, business and communications skills.

To help us all enhance this insight skillset there is a vast body of literature available. But I decided it would be helpful to bring together in one volume the art and science of working in a holistic way to find, tell and action the insight story.

I also wanted to create a book in the form of an easy to access training guide reflecting the way I teach this content in masterclasses and workshops.

This book is primarily for newcomers to customer insight who want a fast track way to becoming a *High Performance Customer Insight Professional*. However, the book should also benefit more experienced insight professionals looking for fresh perspectives.

There is a transformation taking place in the world of insight with technology opening up many new opportunities. It points to a bright future for the insight industry. In the new era, the expertise of the insight professional in understanding what makes people tick and telling the insight story remains critically important.

I hope you enjoy reading what it takes to be a *High Performance Customer Insight Professional*.

If you have any questions about any of the ideas in this book please get in touch.

David Smith

david.smith@dvlsmith.com

INTRODUCTION

Insights into customer behaviour - what customers expect and aspire to - is one of any organisation's most valuable assets. We are now in a new *customer insight era* where the emphasis is on futureproofing organisations - providing strategic foresights that will allow an organisation to adapt to change.

The new insight paradigm retains many of the more traditional legacy skills centred around disciplined thinking. But the new era also calls for an enhanced set of skills.

The emphasis is now on using multiple sources of often imperfect evidence obtained through low-cost techniques, often using fast experimentation. This allows organisations to quickly get feedback on their overall direction of travel and then adapt - course direct - the initial decision in a flexible and pragmatic way.

This new customer insight paradigm requires a mindset that is comfortable with handling ambiguity and compensating for any limitations in the data. It requires someone who is confident in offering a point of view, able to frame the decision choices and to operate in a consultative and creative way.

The High Performance Customer Insight Professional brings together best practice from the insight industry's core legacy skills and combines this with the newer skills needed to make sense of imperfect evidence. This is the platform for communicating the insight message to stakeholders in a way that will achieve actionable outcomes.

This book is structured in three Parts.

Part One - The Insight Sensemaker

We focus on finding the story that exists in the data. Many would-be insight storytellers fall at the first hurdle because they are overwhelmed by the data in front of them. To address this, we introduce our *Seven Analysis Frames* toolkit. This provides an analysis framework to help insight professionals make sense of the complex mix of evidence now available to them.

Part Two - The Insight Story Builder

We look at telling the story. We outline *Seven Story Tools* to help you communicate your insight story to a time-urgent audience. There is much general advice about storytelling, but comparatively little step-by-step instruction on how to build a compelling insight story. This is where our Story Tools will be invaluable.

Part Three - Insights into Action

We provide *Consultancy Strategies* for dealing with different barriers that could block the successful implementation of your insight message. We look at overcoming the resistances that stand in the way of the insight professional persuading senior stakeholders to take action on their insight story.

PART ONE

THE INSIGHT SENSEMAKER

How to make sense of
the insight evidence

The Insight Sensemaker

In Part One we focus on Sensemaking: seeing patterns in a vast ocean of data points and bringing them together into a unifying moment of insight. Today, customer insight professionals need to find the story by synthesising multiple sources of evidence. They need to create a holistic picture by combining different pieces of evidence to unearth compelling insights.

Sensemaking involves knowing how to connect the dots between hard statistical data and softer intuitively generated insights. Isaiah Berlin refers to visionary leaders as having an *acute sense of what fits with what, what springs from what and what leads to what.*

In this part of the book we help the insight professional tackle the challenge of making sense of multiple sources of evidence with our Seven Analysis Frames approach to analysis. This is not a course in data analysis. Our aim is to provide the analyst with key principles - mental models of thinking - that allow them to think *holistically* about their evidence.

The Seven Analysis Frames

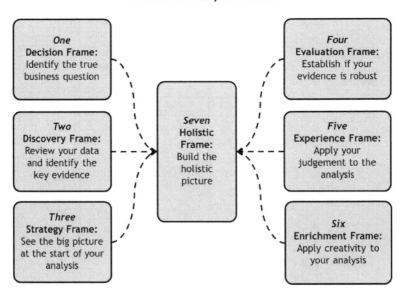

Our Seven Analysis Frames approach

Our Seven Frames approach allows us to break down the holistic analysis process into accessible bite-sized chunks: seven distinct analysis activities. By looking at the evidence one frame at a time, the analyst can examine complex evidence from a number of specific perspectives before arriving at the holistic view - the integrated business story.

How we explain each Frame

We start by outlining the *Guiding Principles* underpinning the frame. We follow this with the *Key Actions* to apply the frame. Next are some *Frequently Asked Questions*. We follow this with a *Top Tip*. Then there is your *Best Next Move* - ideas on applying the frame to your next project. We conclude with a *Summary*.

We now look at the first of our analysis frames - the *Decision Frame*. This will help to ensure you are working on the right problem.

1 THE DECISION FRAME
How to identify the true business question

The *Decision Frame* ensures there is total clarity about the business question. Clearly if there is confusion surrounding what is the true issue to be explored, then it becomes difficult for the customer insight professional to make a successful intervention.

GUIDING PRINCIPLES

Principle One: Begin with the end in mind - unearth the true problem

When analysing data, begin with the end in mind by being clear on the business question you are answering. This reflects one of the key principles in Stephen Covey's *The 7 Habits of Highly Effective People*. It is important that you have identified the problem that lies at the heart of the issue. Do not work on the symptoms of an issue.

Principle Two: Get the helicopter view of the business problem

It is important to understand the wider context - business panorama - in which the business problem is located. Ensure that at all times you have a big picture - helicopter - view of what the project is all about. It is all too easy to get lost in answering specific research questions and fail to focus on the *main thing* the audience expects to do next based on your presentation.

Principle Three: Rigorously explore the stakeholders' real agenda

Make sure you check out all the underlying assumptions that have been made in presenting the initial problem. Ensure that you are not only operating with what has been made *explicit* to you. Work hard to draw out what is *implicit* - what is not being said. Be tenacious in teasing out what may be lurking beneath the surface in the way the business question has been initially presented.

KEY ACTIONS

Action 1: Ensure you are working on the right problem

The creation of a compelling business narrative - and engaging story - hinges on having total clarity around the nature of the business question. Many presentations fail because the insight professional only had a hazy outline of the *true* business question that the project was intended to answer.

In other situations, the true problem may not be identified because the stakeholders are too close to the issue. They have been unable to stand back to see the fuller context and identify all the key concepts and dynamics in play.

For example, the presented problem is that the sales force is not motivated. But the real problem is deficiencies with the product they are trying to sell. Similarly, a presented issue is customers don't understand our new pricing policy. But the true problem may be that customers don't think the company is genuine in its approach to pricing.

There are well-documented factors that get in the way of the true problem - business question - being defined. Learn to recognise these potential danger signs, so you can raise the red flag if you sense these are in play.

Default thinking

One reason why people are working on the wrong problem could be due to the tendency for them to resort to *default thinking*. That is, they think about the problem in the way that they have always done. They do not dig deep to identify what is really at the heart of the problem - the critical underlying issue.

Lego play

Going back a decade or more, Lego found itself a victim of default thinking. Its sales were plateauing which it usually resolved by coming up with ever more ingenious product designs. But this default thinking was no longer working. This led to a decision to identify the more fundamental *phenomenon* underpinning the Lego success story.

After extensive self-examination, Lego realised that at the heart of the Lego success story was the concept of *play*. Once Lego rediscovered *play* as being its raison d'être, the problem moved from *How can we design a new product?* to *How do we reclaim our reputation as the company that knows how children want to play?* Once the company identified that what was important about Lego was the opportunity to play and improvise it was then able to work out strategies to rebuild the Lego legend.

This culminated in *The Lego Movie* which is all about how Lego facilitates play, improvisation and creativity. The theme of the movie was a celebration of Lego's vision and mission: *Inspire and develop the builders of tomorrow!* With *play* being identified as the fundamental *phenomenon* to which they needed to return, Lego was able to continue on its success path.

Critical implicit issues have not been made explicit

Vital pieces of information are often not communicated in the initial briefing because it is assumed that the agency/consultant about to work on the problem must already know these. For example, a research agency is asked by a publisher to do a detailed audit of a competitor. The research study shows that the competitor is performing much better than the client.

The agency gives a rather sheepish presentation, not wanting to upset the client company which does not come out of the research looking good. At the end of the presentation, the audience begin to smile and applaud... Why? Well - the reason for commissioning the research study was that the client was just about to complete the acquisition of this competitor, but the agency had not established this during prior briefings. The lesson here is to ensure everything is made explicit.

There is a flawed underlying assumption

It is possible for an entire project to take place without a critical underlying assumption ever being fully investigated. The consequences can be quite catastrophic. For example, it was assumed that, because Coca-Cola drinkers preferred *New Coke* to *Original Coke* in taste tests, then they would welcome the introduction of new Coke. But in fact, although they liked the taste of new

Coke, some Coca-Cola drinkers resented not having the option of still buying original Coke. The lesson: you always need to establish what evidence exists to support each critical assumption.

Another illustration that highlights the need to always check out the most critical assumptions underpinning an idea comes from the UK TV series *Dragons' Den*. In this show aspiring entrepreneurs present ideas with the hope of securing investment. The programme is littered with examples of projects getting underway without critical assumptions being carefully checked out.

At the top of the list of spectacular flawed assumptions is the idea of supplying drivers with one right-handed glove that they could wear when driving in Europe to remind them to drive on the right side of the road! No one had checked out whether there was a genuine need for this product. This was a *solution* looking for a *problem*!

Big ticket items have been overlooked

One problem definition challenge is that stakeholders can simply miss things. Goethe said, *'The hardest thing to see is what is in front of your eyes'*. We tend to see things not as they are, but as we think they are. Some may recall the Gorilla Experiment. The audience is asked to watch a basketball game and asked to count how many times the ball is thrown by players to other members of their own team.

As a result of concentrating on this task around two thirds fail to spot a person dressed in a gorilla suit who joins the game! So, do not be afraid to ask for clarification of any issue that you feel has not been fully explained.

The problem has been framed in a biased way

Another watch-out is the way the initial problem has been *framed* - positioned. This could provide a selective take on the issue. This may be part of a deliberate attempt to pursue a particular agenda. But often it is due to more unconscious influences.

For instance, a brief that says *as many as 60% said...* creates a different start point from a brief that presents the same piece of evidence as, *as few as 60% said...!* There could also be a predilection towards presenting the optimistic opportunity, as opposed to the more realistic risk focused, perspective (or vice versa).

A tunnel vision, not big picture helicopter, account of the problem

The person initially formulating the problem may be too close to it, and/or not have access to an overall picture of the business challenge. For example, the Head of Operations working for a Local Authority in a seaside town may brief an agency to identify what attractions *day trippers* would like introduced.

However, had the briefing been given by the Chief Executive Officer of the Local Authority, then he/she would explain that the needs of the day trippers must be balanced with the needs of *local residents* who have been lobbying the CEO for better facilities.

Critical complexity has been eliminated or oversimplified

It is unhelpful to include in the briefing process confusing side issues and outlier irrelevances. But it is equally unhelpful to airbrush out of the problem definition stage critical complexities that must be tackled in finding a resolution to the business question. To cite Einstein: *'It is important to make everything as simple as possible - but not simpler'*.

Let us take the example of a car rental firm responding to complaints from customers about the time it takes to rent a car at an airport. The crux of customers' frustration is too much time-consuming paperwork leading to long queues. Addressing the paperwork problem needs to deal with the complexity of there being certain *mandatory* legal checks that must be made by any car hire firm, including ensuring the customer has a valid driving licence.

Here, getting into the detail of what paperwork is mandatory, and what is not, is critical in order to pinpoint practical and actionable ways of streamlining the car rental process.

The scale (quantum) of the issue has not been communicated

Size matters when it comes to defining a problem for someone else to absorb and then develop a solution. A problem generated by a dozen complaints on one specific day is different from a problem that has manifested itself over three months and involves thousands of customers.

Let's take the example of a project triggered by an unacceptable level of customer complaints about a bank's treatment of small businesses. It is important to know whether these are isolated *outlier* complaints or based on a substantive body of complaints pointing to a *systemic* failure in the customer service process.

Naivety about the way the research works

Those inexperienced in commissioning research can be naive about the way people really think and behave and the brief can come across as a *fantasy*. It will catalogue a wish list of ideal requirements.

For example, marketers might like to know exactly how many people would buy the product at price point P, as opposed to price point P+1 and so on. This may be a laudable aspiration, but there are lots of challenges to be addressed, including judging how the competition is likely to react.

Looking at a snapshot in time, not the longer-term trend

Some problems start being defined too early in the process. An issue is spotted, and before it has become a substantive trend, there can be a knee jerk reaction that gets many hares running and projects commissioned.

For example, if a retailer sees a dip in sales of a particular clothing line at the start of the New Year, they could assume that their winter fashion designs are a flop. But, with further investigation, it might have been established that a key competitor, that was in financial difficulty due to poor Christmas sales, has been offering massive January discounts. Thus, the drop in sales was as a result of this seasonal discounting, rather than a problem with the design of the winter range.

Action 2: Ask key stakeholders, and yourself, killer questions to clarify any uncertainty over the business question

A constructive dialogue with stakeholders will help clarify the *true* business question and ensure you are working on the real problem, not the *symptoms*. It is also useful to ask some penetrating questions to help clarify your own thinking.

Einstein's comment about the power of asking questions when solving a problem speaks to this point: *'If I had an hour to solve a problem and my life depended on the solution, I would spend the first 55 minutes determining the proper question to ask, for once I know the proper question, I could solve the problem in less than 5 minutes.'*

Below we look at different categories of question where intelligent probing and questioning of stakeholders - and yourself - will pay dividends. These will help you crystallise the business problem.

Strategy questions - to ensure you are focusing on the business priorities

Fit with business strategy: How does this issue fit with the organisation's wider vision and strategic priorities and business objectives? How will this impact on the delivery of the business objectives?

Clarity on where to play: How does this build us a stronger strategic positioning in where we have chosen to play, and fit with our strategic imperatives?

Clarity on how to win: How does this give us a competitive advantage? How does this help us further understand customer trends, habits and attitudes, needs and tensions?

Clarity on how to get there: How novel, original or different is this idea - what is the precise competitive advantage we will gain over competitors by doing this? Exactly how does this help us deliver our strategy?

Appreciation of competitive dynamics: What is the most likely competitive response to our proposed action?

Understanding longer term consumer trends: How does this fit with what we know about the most important consumer trends?

Outcome questions - to keep the end in mind and know what needs to be achieved

Purpose and intention: How does this issue impact on the fundamental business and commercial goals of the organisation? What are the implications of saying *No* to the stated request and seeking a redefined problem?

Expected actions: What difference do you expect to be able to make by undertaking this project? What decisions do you expect to be able to make because you now have this data?

Forward plan: What is it that you will now do with the results? What are the *What If* scenarios for different outcomes and what would you do in these different scenarios?

What is at stake for the stakeholder: What is the biggest single risk, and most major opportunity, associated with this venture?

Success: What would success look like for the project, the business and its stakeholders? What is the size of the prize? What are the consequences for the business? How will this impact on growth and profitability?

Blocks and barriers: What is stopping us from moving forward now? What information or insight are we missing to help with our decision-making and plans?

Judgement questions - to help find the sweet spot between gut feel instinct and the evidence

The common sense test: What do we already know about this, could we sort this problem from first principles? Is the customer voice the most illuminating intelligence for this - who else could you ask for insight?

The risk and opportunity assessment: Have you identified the biggest risk for the business and also the biggest opportunity?

The likelihood of success assessment: What is the biggest barrier to the proposed initiative working?

The What's Next test: If we conducted this study/obtained this data, would it help us to know what we should be doing next?

Alignment on the issue: How much do you personally agree with the view of stakeholders that the key issue we should be investigating is X (a summary of the emerging key factors)?

Your view: If you were the sole/only person totally in charge of sorting out this challenge/issue - what would you yourself do next to find out what is going on?

Context questions - to get a big picture view of the issue

The big picture: What is it that you currently do not know that you believe you must know in order to identify the true *phenomenon* at the heart of the business problem that - when understood - will make for an informed decision?

How did we get here? Would you walk me through how you arrived at this request for X?

Who has been involved and what was the trigger? Who is involved in this decision, who is the ultimate decision-maker, and to whom will the project results then be delivered and when - what are they expecting from this study of customers?

How it squares - fits - with what we know? On what basis have we arrived at this view? Just how rigorous was the hypothesis generation process? Have stakeholders checked out the defining assumptions which underpin the claimed position?

Supporting evidence: You are saying that X is based on an assumption that everybody wants to achieve Y. What evidence do you have to back up this assumption? Could I check the exact source of this critical statistic that is pivotal to your argument?

Key assumptions: Please explain how you arrived at making the assumption that X would lead to Y?

Stakeholder agenda questions - to help identify the different agendas in play

Briefing dysfunctionalities: Who is involved in the decision-making and how do they see the problem? What is each person's real agenda, concern or challenge? What is not being made explicit?

The personality dimension: Is this project primarily about progressing an individual's agenda rather than what is best for the organisation?

Framing biases: You have introduced X in the following way: would you say that most people would see X in that way?

Methodological biases: Could I check, on balance what is your preference when it comes to the *evidence* for informed decision-making - qualitative, quantitative or both?

Insight research naivety: Is this *comfort* research - providing a safety blanket - or will the findings genuinely impact on the final decision?

Political agendas: Is your analysis of the situation likely to be fully accepted by others - are there any potential objectors?

Deep dive questions - to get beneath the surface

Test the core unifying idea to destruction: Test the underlying drivers of the idea. On a scale of 1 to 10 (where 1 is unsure and 10 is totally sure) how sure are you that you have identified the underlying core drivers of what is causing this issue/challenge?

Test critical assumptions: Exactly how did you test to destruction the assumption that X will lead to Y?

Validate key statistics and evidence: Check the key statistics and evidence for any hypotheses. Could I check the source for statistic X? Why do you believe this statistic is needed?

Test actionability - explore if insight works in this way: Please explain how getting this insight on customer behaviour will allow us to influence/change what they do?

Identify gaps: Are there any information needs or omissions that need plugging? In an ideal world what information would you most like to know?

Check understanding - all wording, terminology and language: Could I clarify and confirm your understanding of the word X - could you please tell me exactly what you mean by this?

Practicalities questions - to check out exactly how the intended project will work

Timetable: When are the findings required for decision-making - can the project be completed within this timeframe?

Acceptable quality: What type of evidence will be accepted by the audience as credible for decision-making - can this standard be achieved?

Within budget: What is the budget for the project - is this realistic for the outcomes that are expected?

Operational practicality: Are there any barriers or obstacles that could undermine the execution of this project?

Fit with organisational culture: Is this project aligned with the way the organisation operates?

Compliance: Does this project comply with the law, ESOMAR/Market Research Society Codes of Conduct? Is it ethical, legal and compatible with professional standards?

Use powerful questioning techniques for your briefing questions

The questions provided above will help you gain a better understanding of the true problem. But, often, the *way* you ask the question will be critical to securing helpful answers. You need questioning techniques to overcome any resistances stakeholders may have to your questions.

Below there are some questioning styles to help you crystallise the true business question and fix any gaps in your thinking about the problem.

Challenge beliefs

Challenge the rationale and underlying assumptions of an argument. For example: What you are saying is based on the assumption that everyone is concerned about animal welfare. What evidence do you have to back this up?

Be a pedant

Assess the accuracy of each fact. For example: Could I just check the precise source for this statistic?

Make views concrete

Go beyond general statements. For instance: You say people no longer trust the police. Does this mean you would never report a crime that happened to you?

Clarify

Listen, then clarify what has been said by feeding this back in a precise way to check everyone is on the same page. For example: I understand you to be saying that you will never use the X hotel chain in future. Could I check - is this the point you are trying to get over?

Focus

Ask detailed questions to establish the exact novelty, originality and impact of the issue. For example: If we did this, could you pinpoint the precise way in which we would gain a competitive advantage over our next biggest competitor?

Identity risk

Ask whether any formal risk assessment has been conducted around the idea. For example: What is the biggest single risk associated with this venture?

Play devil's advocate

Offer the opposing point of view and test for reaction. For instance: You believe that wind farms are better than nuclear energy plants, but a lot of people think that wind farms are a blot on the landscape.

Think quantum

Probe the scale, depth and importance of the issue. For example: You say we must protect tigers and lions in travelling circuses - how many such animals are there in the UK? (If the answer is 25 then the strategy you would pursue would be different from if the answer is 1,000!)

Ladder-up to key concepts

Take the immediate functional issue and ladder up to the bigger concept/emotional benefit at the heart of this issue. For example: in exploring how much people will pay for vitamin tablets, frame this around helping people to achieve high energy levels - attain their life goals.

Apply outside-in thinking

Encourage the person not to think *inside-out* but *outside-in* - from the *third corner*. For example: If a Man from Mars arrives and sees a bank charging its customers for looking after their own funds, what would he say?

Scenarios and game theory

Set up different scenarios and enquire about these. For example: If we change the connector on the next version of this product, how do you think our competitors will respond?

Think differently

You could try gamification techniques. For instance: If we ran a competition to find out who in the organisation knows most about this problem, who would win - and why?

Wave a magic wand

Set up a scenario whereby there were no constraints or resource issues. Explore ideally what they would like to achieve. For example: If you could wave a magic wand, tell me what the end outcome of this project would look like?

Make it personal

Reduce the argument down to the individual's own world. For example: What would you do next if it was your own money?

Action 3: Be a Business Question Translator - getting from the business question to the business solution

At the start, get a mental picture of how your project is going to *work*. Being able to think through in advance the journey from the business question to the solution will pay dividends. It is helpful to think of the insight professional's role as being a *Business Question Translator*.

The Business Question Translation Process

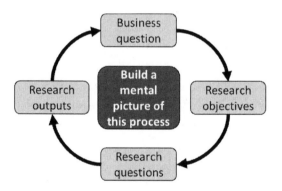

Start with a clear understanding of the *business question*. Translate this into the *research objectives* that must be met to answer this business question. Then decide on the *research questions* you need to ask. Next anticipate the likely response to these questions - the *research outputs*. Then be clear on how these research outputs will address the business question. Having this picture in your head in advance will put you in the driving seat when it comes to building your storyline.

Action 4: Be totally clear about the project outcome

One of the goals of Decision Frame thinking is to get clarity around the type of outcome/decision that will conclude the project. Key fundamental outcome scenarios include:

A go/no-go decision

There is the demanding situation where your evidence will be used to make a *go/no-go* or *yes/no* decision. Here, there are no shades of grey. As the insight professional, you are being asked to say whether you are for or against an idea. These are the go/green-light or no-go/red-light decisions. For example, should a UK finance organisation, given trends in global finance, now switch its Head Office from London to Frankfurt or not?

Directional guidance - where course correction is possible

There are scenarios where there is the flexibility to adapt the final decision en route. You are asked to provide an overall direction of travel based on the research. But importantly, there is the opportunity to *course correct* this decision as more information becomes available. Thus, if the initial recommendation is slightly off-course, there are still opportunities to retrieve the situation. For example: what are the best types of advertisement to use on an online retailer's redesigned website.

Generating new ideas and clarifying thinking

There will be decision scenarios where there is no clear-cut decision being made one way or the other. The project has been devised to clarify people's thinking around possible options and/or trigger new ideas. So here, arguably, there is less pressure around the decision. For example, this could be preliminary research to generate initial ideas for enhancing an in-store customer retail experience.

Questions to identify the category of outcome - type of decision - being made

Below we provide some questions you can ask to bring greater clarity around the specific type of decision being made.

Business impact: To what degree will this decision influence key business metrics, such as annual turnover or profit levels?

Decision-making flexibility: To what extent will there be an opportunity to adjust the initial decision on a rolling basis as the initiative progresses?

Link to organisational values: Is this a decision that relates to the core espoused values of the organisation? For example, if a company has publicly dedicated itself to maintaining high environmental standards, then the decisions and actions it takes with regard to waste disposal will be subject to greater scrutiny than other companies.

Whether an evidence-based or intuition culture: Is this decision likely to be dominated by a culture of evidence-based decision-making or one that will rely mainly on stakeholders' intuition, beliefs, feelings and/or vision?

Degree of media attention: Is this a decision where the outcome will be played out in the public domain under intense media scrutiny, or is this a low-profile issue? (A decision to sponsor a UK Premiership superstar footballer will receive different attention than the sponsorship of a minor league hockey club player).

Personal agendas: To what extent is this decision linked to high-profile stakeholders who are committed to particular outcomes?

Action 5: Identify how your research evidence is likely to be received

Ask questions of stakeholders to get a sense of how the findings are likely to be received. At the start of your analysis process you need to know the scrutiny to which your evidence could be subjected. At the very outset of a project, put yourself into the shoes of your stakeholder - the end decision-maker.

Questions to ask about the project

¤ Will the study be accepted by your decision-making audience? By accepted we mean will it square with their view of the world and be considered? Or will it be rejected out of hand (the bring me more acceptable findings syndrome!)?

- Will the results be delivered within the timescale for effective decision-making to take place?

- Will the evidence be seen as being of sufficient quality to aid the decision-making process? Specifically, is the evidence you are providing fit-for-purpose for the decisions being made: is it providing evidence that is robust and credible? Is the evidence valid, reliable and generalisable? Are there any gaps in the evidence, and do you, as the presenter, have any doubts about the data?

Further issues to explore to assess how well your evidence will be received

- Are there any concealed agendas or deep-seated prejudices in play around this business question that could deflect or derail the presentation?

- Do you sense the audience - in evaluating the evidence - will or will not strike the right balance between their System 1 (more intuitive) and System 2 (more rational) thinking?

- Are there any resistances around different types of methodological evidence that are likely to get in the way of a finding being accepted? Is there any resistance or nervousness with statistics and/or a concern about the robustness of qualitative research?

Action 6: Minimise mission drift and the impact of events

The skilled researcher will anticipate where there may be a *drift* in the initially declared objectives of the project and/or the arrival of *events* that could impact the project. Some key questions you might want to ask stakeholders in order to minimise mission drift are outlined below.

Questions to help anticipate how the project might change direction

- Is there likely to be any reframing of the project objectives?

- How likely is it that the project objectives will be re-prioritised?

- What are the uncontrollable factors that could affect the project - macro/global issues such as movements in the exchange rate and so on?

¤ What are the controllable factors that could change during the project, such as the product offer or pricing policy and so on?

¤ What is the likely competitive response to new initiatives that needs to be factored into the project?

¤ Are there any potential disruptors or wild card factors that could affect the project - is it possible to make an assessment of their impact on the project?

¤ How likely is it that on this topic there could be a sudden change in consumer behaviour - how customers might think and act - that needs to be factored into your approach?

FREQUENTLY ASKED QUESTIONS

Question One: Surely in many situations, the customer insight professional is being told to answer a specified question and it would be difficult for them to ask all the questions outlined above in order to get to the heart of the true problem?

> **Answer:** It is true that in many stakeholder/internal insight professional relationships, and also client/agency relationships, there is often a strong imperative around answering a specified predetermined question. But if you want to end up with an effective business solution you need to be strong about exploring what is really going on.

Question Two: If you have answered the research objectives related to the business question, surely this is sufficient for the customer insight professional? It is up to the decision-makers to work out what this means in answering the business question.

> **Answer:** Today the expectation is that the customer insight professional will be able to relate the research evidence to the business question. So, if the business question is should we buy company X? it is insufficient to just deal with one of the research objectives, such as the level of customer satisfaction with company X - always focus on answering the business question.

Question Three: If you sense there is drift taking place from the original objective of a project towards another agenda, how do you deal with this?

Answer: Do not assume everything will magically correct itself, instead make your concerns explicit - raise a red flag and get a dialogue going with your stakeholders around your concerns.

 Top Tip

Be tenacious and persistent in getting to the heart of the true business problem. Take personal responsibility for, and invest energy in, clarifying any issues that you sense have not been fully unearthed or explored. If these are not clarified, this could undermine your effectiveness in solving the business question.

 Best Next Move

Identify the three killer questions you will ask your key stakeholders - and the particular questioning techniques/styles you will employ - to ensure you are working on the real problem, not the symptom! (These questions could be asked as part of the initial briefing on the project, or at a point prior to starting the analysis.)

SUMMARY

The Decision Frame is about identifying the true business problem. Always *begin with the end in mind* - with a picture of the final decision that needs to be made.

Focus on the core concept - *phenomenon* - underpinning the business challenge: avoid lazy *default thinking*.

Be forensic and imaginative in the range of questions you ask to get to the true problem.

Be a *Business Question Translator*:

Understand how the business question translates into the research objectives.

Translate these into questions you may wish to ask.

Reflect on how the answers to these questions will inform the business decision.

Be clear on the type of decision that will be made at the end of the project.

Anticipate any likely mission drift.

Next we look at the *Discovery Frame*. This is about making sure you have organised your data, have a sense of its robustness, and are beginning to fashion your storyline around the key evidence.

2 THE DISCOVERY FRAME
How to review your data and identify the key evidence

The *Discovery Frame* is about reviewing the available evidence and determining its overall robustness prior to more detailed analysis.

GUIDING PRINCIPLES

Principle One: Be clear on the different genres of evidence - and its robustness - available to answer the business question

You need to organise your evidence according to type, then get a sense of its robustness as a prelude to prioritising the most compelling data.

Principle Two: Focus on the most compelling evidence that will drive your story - your business solution

Identify and keep at the front of your mind what pieces of evidence will best answer the business question. Begin to zero in on the critical data that will drive your evidence-based storyline.

Principle Three: Assemble the mix of evidence most likely to tap into how people think, feel and act

Begin to assemble evidence that will engage your audience at three levels. First, relate to how they *think* about the issue. Secondly, tap into their intuition - how people *feel* about this issue at an emotional level. Finally, identify evidence that involves them and helps them take *action* in relation to what you are saying.

KEY ACTIONS

Action 1: Organise the evidence into categories to smooth the analysis process

It is easy to become overwhelmed by the data: information overload and data paralysis can set in. Start to unlock the meaning in the data by classifying your evidence. Below is a simple, illustrative taxonomy to help classify the different types of data available on your project to create your story.

A taxonomy for classifying insight evidence

Secondary data: Existing evidence collected by a third-party source, often for another purpose, but which can be applied to your project.

Ethnographic/observation data: Evidence collected in situ through observation. The observer may be a non-participant or be participating in the event under observation.

Qualitative evidence: Evidence collected from small samples of individuals in a flexible way (the researcher will decide what to probe next, based on previous answers, which is in contrast to quantitative research which follows a standardised question order).

Quantitative evidence: This covers data collected using larger survey samples either in face-to-face, telephone or online modes.

Social media listening: Data that has been generated on social media platforms can be analysed using, for example, *sentiment analysis* which classifies evidence into what is positive, neutral or negative.

Passive data: Insights that can be gleaned by, for example, examining an individual's website behaviour (which has to be subject to data privacy rules and codes of conduct).

Financial data: There will be data that allows you, for example, to assess the profitability of particular target segments.

Customer transaction data: We now arrive at the opportunities the customer insight professional has to utilise the data an organisation holds about its customers' transactions.

Action 2: Assess the overall robustness of the evidence

Let's look at the key criteria to assess the evidence for robustness: validity, reliability and generalisability.

Validity

An opening evaluation step is to assess evidence against its *face validity*. How well does a particular piece of data stand up when assessed against: what *clues* are available about the issue; what *anecdotal* evidence exists about this topic; and what *archetypal* evidence is surfacing?

Clues: A piece of data that was gathered for a different purpose than the one under investigation, but nevertheless may provide some insight on the veracity of a point being made.

Anecdotal evidence: Evidence taken from a few individuals that, although not providing a full coherent story of the topic under investigation, nevertheless rings true and begins to provide some initial insights.

Archetypal evidence: A piece of evidence that is consistent with other sources of evidence - and prior knowledge - and is therefore suggesting some fundamental truth or observation that helps to understand the issue being explored.

Construct validity

At the next level, the analyst may examine the authoritative evidence for its construct validity: that is the extent to which the evidence is based on a research process that measures what it is intending to measure. It is about ensuring the results are free from systematic bias.

For example, a study aims to explore the attitudes of a nationally representative sample of individuals towards public transport provision. Here, the results would be invalid if those who had not travelled on public transport in the last three months were excluded. Their decision not to travel may reflect dissatisfaction with the public transport provision: these views should be reflected in the customer satisfaction study.

Assessing the validity of qualitative evidence

Grounded Theory provides a framework for addressing the validity of qualitative evidence. It can be shown empirically that, once around 30 individuals have been questioned on any one topic, the most critical attitudinal and behavioural dimensions associated with an issue can be identified.

For example, in exploring people's attitudes towards a local bus service, 30 regular travellers would provide a comprehensive picture of the good and bad points of the bus service. With this sample size, it is not possible to measure the relative importance of each issue. But this size of sample would be sufficient to alert decision-takers to any fundamental problems or major shortcomings with the service.

It is important to get this point over to senior management who often feel that many thousands of interviews are needed before it is legitimate to make a substantive point.

Reliability

Another dimension against which to assess robustness is reliability. This refers to whether evidence collected to examine a business question holds good over time. Clearly, we do not want evidence that is only valid for the particular moment in time when that evidence was collected.

If, for example, the evidence collected about attitudes towards Brighton as a holiday resort was taken on a freak summer's day when there were unseasonably low temperatures, then there are risks in using this evidence as a guide to what people think of this seaside town as a potential holiday resort.

The reliability/validity relationship

It is important to recognise that reliability operates hand-in-hand with validity. Clearly if we had a measure that is reliable, in the sense that it produces consistent results over time, but it fails to pass the validity test, then this is not reassuring. Equally if we had a *valid* measure - one that does measure what we are supposed to be measuring - but is not *reliable* (does not hold good over time) we would be similarly concerned.

Generalisability

Another dimension of robustness is generalisability. This concept helps us understand the extent to which the research conditions under which the evidence was collected is typical of the commercial environment in which this product or service will be used.

Let's take an example of assessing views on the ease of preparing a new type of pre-prepared meal. If you researched this by setting up an experiment in a fully equipped state-of-the-art test kitchen, it may be risky to assume that the research findings reflect how the new product would perform in a typical family kitchen.

Clearly there is a trade-off between enjoying the benefits of undertaking research in a controlled environment and testing in a way that reflects the realities of a social and/or commercial setting.

Action 3: Reduce the data mass to identify the most meaningful evidence

When it comes to reducing the data down to the killer evidence that will drive your storyline, it helps to start by applying a number of simple data reduction techniques. These are simple techniques that can be applied to reduce the sheer volume of the data. This will make it easier for all concerned to understand.

20 data reduction tips

Cut the data mass: This includes reducing, where appropriate, decimal places and unnecessary percentage signs.

Percentages not numbers: Do not show numbers *and* percentages together as this creates a number-heavy table.

The base for percentages: Provide the base for all percentages, including specifying whether the base is weighted or not.

Combine subgroups: Where subgroups are not telling a different story, consider combining these.

Re-order information: A computer table may show regions in alphabetical order, but this does not mean that you have to present them this way. Group data in the way that is most meaningful in developing your story.

Use re-percentaging: Re-percentage data on a more relevant base in order to clarify the point you are making.

Use measures of location: Use averages (mean, median and mode) in order to summarise the data.

Simply explain measures of variation: Use measures of standard deviation but make these explanations user-friendly.

Ensuring rows and columns add to 100%: Clarify where columns and rows should and should not add to 100%, explaining the situation if not.

Clarify Don't Knows and Not Answered: With survey data, there is often confusion about which questions were *not answered*, as opposed to those questions to which the person *did not know the answer*.

Weighting: Explain where a weighted base has been used.

Slide/table labelling: Ensure there is consistency between the labelling of the question on your presentation table and the question wording used in the survey. If the question was *Are you satisfied with company X's performance?* the table should *not* be labelled as *Customer's happiness with the company*. Satisfaction and happiness are different concepts.

Contextual norms and related evidence: Include norms that help us understand a particular statistic. For example, if you showed how many miles a particular footballer ran in a Premiership football game, it would be helpful to know the average distance run in a typical game.

Self-explanatory titles: All table titles should be clear to even someone who does not understand the background to the study.

Provide short summaries: Provide short descriptions of what each part of the table is saying.

Accurate labelling of concepts: The words for a label used in your table may have been drawn from the questionnaire, but this may not always be the best way of getting over your point. So, relabel as needed whilst staying true to the core concept.

Remove any noise that hinders comprehension: Sometimes computer programs automatically put percentages below each *column*, even though the percentage is based on each *row*. Sort out these details to help immediate comprehension.

Signal key information: Different devices, such as shading and icons, can be used to focus the audience on the key data.

Highlighting key data: Use different icons and design ideas to highlight and showcase key data.

Make use of white space: White space and dotted/emboldened lines all help to make the data clearer.

Action 4: Review the statistical techniques available to aid the analysis

The Seven Analysis Frames approach is not intended to be a statistical analysis course. But we have included a guide to the types of techniques you might want to apply to your data.

An overview of levels of statistical analysis

Some of the available statistical techniques are classified below. Here we would suggest that you talk to statistical colleagues about how to apply certain techniques.

The ordering of the data: Applying simple data reduction techniques in order to see visually and intuitively key data.

Cross tabulation: Looking at how a key finding varies by different customer subgroups.

Measures of location: Techniques to summarise the typical average or most frequent occurrences.

Measures of variation: Looking at the variation around the key statistic.

Measures of difference/significance: Using tests of significance to tell us whether we are working with random numbers or something that is substantive.

Measures of correlation/association: Seeing to what extent there is a relationship with, for example, sales and advertising spend.

Visual mapping techniques: Displaying the data visually to further enhance our ability to look at relationships and patterns.

Prioritisation of needs: This includes various conjoint analysis techniques that allow us to identify what are the most important factors in driving consumer preference.

Segmentation: The use of factor and cluster analysis to identify how groups of customers differ from each other on critical dimensions.

Forecasting: Drawing together data into observations, identifying themes and then trends which we may then extrapolate into the future.

Complement the application of statistical tests to your evidence by applying common sense analysis principles.

- ¤ Ensure that the *statistically significant* evidence is also *relevant* to answering the business question. The experienced analyst is looking for substantive, relevant and significant findings.
- ¤ Ask if this statistical finding fits into the broader pattern of supporting evidence surrounding this point.
- ¤ Establish whether this statistical finding is intuitively explainable - does it make sense given what is known.

Action 5: Focus on the Must-know not Nice-to-have information

With most business presentations, the essence of the story can be told using only 20% of the available evidence. Be ruthless in identifying this 20% of data that is most critical in answering the business question.

Apply the What's in it for Me? test

Apply the *What's in it for Me* (WIIFM) test: look at the evidence through the lens of the audience - focus on evidence that provides *actionable substance*. Ask yourself whether or not each piece of evidence is telling you something new and/or different that is actionable? Is this evidence that can be constructively applied to change behaviour around the issue under investigation?

Apply the So What? and Now What? tests

Asking the *So What?* question of each piece of data will also help ensure you are answering the business question, not simply providing general information not relevant to the business challenge? In addition, asking the *Now What?* question will help guide you to evidence the audience is likely to find actionable.

Questions to help you focus on the killer evidence

- Does this evidence help us directly answer the key business and/or research objective?
- Is this information I must know about to answer this business question (as opposed to information that is only nice to know)?
- Does this tell me anything new? Is this what I already know?
- Does this data specifically address a key issue underpinning the entire purpose of the whole presentation?
- Does this data plug a critical gap in the existing information that is vital to help the audience arrive at their final decision?
- Does this enrich the depth of our insight? Does this data provide us with a fresh, previously not understood, insight about a critical issue?
- Is this evidence believable?
- Does this piece of evidence draw attention to what is at stake here for the audience?
- Does this new or previously unknown fact help us understand how to change behaviour?
- Does this piece of data support a specific call to action or recommendation or the framing of a decision choice?

Further questions to help you identify the key evidence

- Is this data the audience is expecting?
- Will this evidence *touch the world* of key stakeholders and influence how they think about the business question?
- Is this data that will support their likely decision?
- Will this be of interest or provide a helpful insight for the key audience stakeholders?
- What impact will this insight have on the profitability of the organisation?
- Does this evidence help simplify a complex issue (or is it simply adding confusion)?
- Does this help provide wider business context for understanding the true business question?

- ¤ Is this a core relevant point of view or an outlier that does not fit in with the main body of evidence?

- ¤ Does this evidence challenge existing beliefs and misconceptions in a way that helps to identify a new insight?

- ¤ Is this evidence saying something about changing consumer behaviour that would help answer the business question?

Ensure your evidence will answer key stakeholder questions

Ensure that the evidence is sufficiently comprehensive to answer stakeholders' questions. These are questions that, if not answered, could undermine the credence and acceptability of the project.

Is the level of precision right?

Ask whether you have the *precision* that will be required to satisfy key stakeholders? For example, if you are measuring the efficacy of a pharmaceutical treatment, then high levels of precision are required. But, if you are looking for feedback to aid the creative juices on what people think about a new design for a magazine, then a different level of precision is required.

Are you providing the depth of understanding expected?

It is important to be able to answer critical *Why* questions - you need to explain why people behave in a particular way. Ask yourself whether there is sufficient depth of understanding to reassure stakeholders? Saying that X is true, but not being able to explain why this is the case, is not very reassuring.

Have you ensured there are no critical evidence gaps in the solution?

Constantly revisit the business question: ask yourself whether the types of evidence you are assembling answer the business question. You do not want to be at the end of your analysis only to realise that there are evidence gaps and critical questions still left to answer.

Action 6: Provide a powerful mix of evidence

We have introduced the idea of engaging your audience by establishing how they will be thinking, feeling and are likely to act in relation to your narrative. It pays dividends to look at the evidence you will need to tap into your audience's emotions and get buy-in to your central narrative.

Provide the right blend of rational and more emotive evidence that addresses how the audience thinks, feels and is likely to act. Identify the blend of evidence required to answer the business question and engage the audience.

Provide statistical arguments that will strike a chord with those who are looking for rational arguments that relate to the way they think. But accompany this with qualitative evidence that will engage the audience at an emotional level. In addition, provide evidence that will gain buy-in and encourage the audience to take action.

FREQUENTLY ASKED QUESTIONS

Question One: What if, as part of the Discovery Frame phase, you realise that you do not fully understand the business question that led to the commissioning of the original project?

> **Answer:** Ideally the crystallisation of the business problem is resolved at the start - *Decision Framing phase* - of the project. But often there remains a lack of clarity even though the project is underway. Constantly loop back to stakeholders - asking the key questions outlined in the Decision Frame - to make sure you are absolutely clear on the *true* business question.

Question Two: How can you begin to identify what is the most robust evidence in relation to the business question if you have yet to get really underway with an in-depth and detailed analysis of the data?

> **Answer:** It is true that the robustness of certain evidence may not be established until you enter into detailed data analysis. But the Discovery Frame will begin to give you a sense of where the most potent evidence lies.

Question Three: Isn't the Discovery Frame stage too early in the process to begin to think about how the evidence will be assembled into the final storyline - business solution?

> **Answer:** A major analysis principle we have promoted is *always to begin with the end in mind*. So, it makes perfect sense to think about possible storylines early in the process. You will, of course, rigorously review your initial storytelling position but, by beginning with the end in mind, you

are more likely to end up with a presentation that meets audience expectations.

 Top Tip

Be energetic and committed to the task of identifying that critical 20% of the evidence that drives your storyline. It is easy to think that, because the client has paid for all the data, it is your duty to present everything back to them. This lazy thinking is always a mistake. Pascal said, *'I apologise for this long letter, but I didn't have the time to write a shorter one'.*

 Best Next Move

On your next project identify the strongest *mix* of quantitative and qualitative (rational and more emotively focused) evidence you will bring together in order to successfully deliver your message. Keep this in mind and review as your analysis progresses.

SUMMARY

The *Discovery Frame* is about reviewing and prioritising the evidence and beginning to see the wood for the trees. It is about reducing the data down to tell the story using only around 20% of the evidence.

Make an initial assessment of the validity, reliability and generalisability of your key evidence.

Be clear on when you will rely on more statistical techniques to unearth the meaning and relevance of the data, and where you will rely more on your own judgement and experience.

Recognise that to communicate your message you need evidence that will tap into the way people think, feel and are likely to act in relation to your message.

Next, we look at the *Strategy Frame*. This ensures you have an overarching strategy in place before you begin your detailed analysis. This will help you avoid data overwhelm.

3 THE STRATEGY FRAME
How to see the big picture at the start of your analysis

The *Strategy Frame* is about developing an overall analysis strategy to ensure the analyst does not get lost in the detail. It is about getting above the parapet and seeing the big picture - storyline - in play.

With a clear strategy, the analysis process becomes a rewarding journey, rather than a thankless task involving wading through endless amounts of information and running the risk of analysis paralysis.

Analysis is not simply studying the first data table, immersing yourself in this, and then moving on to the next. You need to step back and have a plan to ensure you first obtain an understanding of the overall big picture.

GUIDING PRINCIPLES

Principle One: Identify the big picture before starting the detailed analysis

There is no one right analysis approach. It is a personal decision. Different individuals will work with the data in different ways. It is clearly inappropriate to be prescriptive in recommending a detailed, specific way of analysing data.

However, one approach to consider is to think of analysis as gradually moving from a big picture overview to a more detailed understanding. This is an analysis strategy that helps to avoid getting lost in the data and/or overwhelmed by the analysis process.

Principle Two: Put game changing insight at the heart of your storyline

Successful insight presentations require genuine insights to be at their core. A lot of insight presentations fail because the analyst is trying to retrieve a flawed starting position. They have never pinpointed a true insight to be at the heart of their story. This requires having total clarity around what is an *insight* and what is not.

An insight is *not* simply a piece of mildly interesting information. An insight is not just reporting an attitude or a piece of behaviour. It is about pinpointing exactly how an attitude motivates and drives a potential change in behaviour.

A true insight needs a *psychological* dimension that tells us something about people's motivations, attitudes and feelings. It will also have a *behavioural* dimension that allows us to relate this motivation or understanding to how individuals are likely to behave in relation to a particular issue or business question.

Principle Three: Begin to get a sense of possible storylines at the start of the process

At an early stage in the analysis process start to explore the different storylines that are emerging in answering the business question.

KEY ACTIONS

Action 1: Start with a big picture overview of the evidence

The hallmark of an experienced analyst is the ability to quickly get to the big picture view, whilst having the flexibility of mind to constantly test to destruction this initial view as the analysis progresses.

Have a core unifying idea

Successful, productive, creative individuals tend to start with a clear vision of the overall end product - whether this is a piece of art or a novel that they want to create. They are very clear about their *core unifying idea*. And it is not until this *vision* is in place that they will then start looking at the detail and nuances around this big idea.

Get the Helicopter view first

There is a strong case for the analyst to quickly obtain a sense of the overall *big picture* storyline *before* getting into the detail. Rapidly getting the high-level *helicopter* view will minimise the risk of getting lost in the minutiae of the data. Start with a big picture view but be prepared to refine and/or revise your initial thinking.

This big picture first approach is underpinned by how datasets often *work*. In a high proportion of scenarios, looking at the total story by different subgroups will add nuances but not change the fundamental storyline. The *total sample* storyline will only be *refined* by the subsequent exploration of the detail.

However, in a small proportion of cases, the initial total sample analysis could be *suppressing* important storylines that will only be revealed by detailed subgroup analysis. There is a possibility that, within an overall total sample story, there could be two or more fundamentally different stories being suppressed.

Successive waves of analysis

Think of the analysis process as shuttling between the emerging big picture story and the detail to arrive at the best overall narrative. It is about *successive waves* of analysis. This process of looping around from big picture to small detail, then back to big picture is referred to as the *Hermeneutic Circle* process.

Meeting student expectations

Let's take the example of a study to look at students' attitudes towards their university experience. We learn that the overwhelming majority (nine in ten of all students) felt the university *was meeting their expectations*. Here, it is unlikely that, as we explore variations by those studying the arts rather than the sciences, we would detect a major departure from this overall finding. The analysis by subject, and other subgroup variables, would simply refine the central storyline - the university is meeting expectations.

Action 2: Play to your personal analysis strengths

Choosing an analytical process to follow is a personal decision. It is important to develop an analysis strategy that plays to your strengths and is one with which you feel comfortable.

Deductive and inductive analysis

For some people, their first reflex is to follow the *deductive* thinking approach to analysis. They will work through the evidence in a logical way to arrive at a conclusion by testing hypotheses. Others will favour the *inductive* approach, whereby they look at data points and develop these into an explanatory theory.

Some will feel comfortable adding *convergent* thinking styles to their analysis style. They will zero in on the originally defined problem and focus their solutions around this. In contrast, there will be those who favour *divergent* thinking. They think flexibly and laterally around the original problem and see where this takes them.

There is no one right way to analyse data. The experienced analyst often brings into play a mix of analytical approaches when analysing their evidence - a *holistic* approach.

Evidence-driven not theory-led

Be alert to the danger of your analysis becoming seduced by a grand theory to the point that you start, possibly subconsciously, *selectively* looking for evidence that supports this theory. In doing so, you become blind to counter evidence that does not support the theory. This results in the eventual story being presented being too theory-led with the data being fitted in to make the storyline work. This is not good practice. The goal is to create a story built out of the constant *testing* of the robustness of your emerging storyline against the evidence.

Action 3: Use a mix of qualitative and quantitative modes of analysis

The holistic analyst will look at their evidence through both the qualitative and quantitative lenses. We need to remember that there are not just qualitative and quantitative *methods* of data collection, there are also qualitative and quantitative *modes* of analysing data.

Qualitative and quantitative methods and modes of analysis

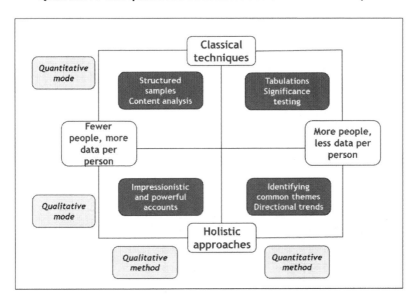

Thus, in creating an integrated story from multiple data sources, it is important to make sure that your *quantitative* data is analysed using both *quantitative* and *qualitative modes* of analysis. This will add further depth of understanding to your findings.

For example, the *statistical* analysis of customer satisfaction survey data may clearly identify that the majority of visitors to a hotel are dissatisfied with their experience. But, with a more in-depth contextual *qualitative mode of analysis*, it will be possible to unearth what is driving this dissatisfaction.

Similarly, on occasions, it can be helpful to provide a *quantitative* analysis of qualitative evidence, even though it is based on small numbers. For example, it could be helpful to spell out that *28 out of 30 people liked design X*, rather than just saying, *the majority liked X.*

Action 4: Work with a genuine insight capable of driving your storyline

The effective customer insight professional needs to have a forensic understanding of precisely how a particular insight works - how it is capable of changing consumer behaviour.

Insight requires a psychological and behavioural dimension

We introduced the point earlier that a true insight must contain two critical dimensions:

¤ A *psychological* dimension: it needs to describe what is inside the customer's mind - their causal motivations, attitudes, beliefs and feelings.

¤ A *behavioural* dimension: it needs to describe what is observable - what the customer is or is not doing as a result of these causal psychological factors.

An insight needs to reveal a link between these two dimensions: causal psychological factors and behaviour. An actionable insight is one that can create change or reinforce an intended customer attitude, belief or feeling in a way that strengthens a brand. Powerful insights often reflect an unresolved *tension* in the mind of the customer and, as such, have the power and momentum, to drive action.

Insights are created not found

It is important to remember that powerful insights are not *found*, they are *created* through a strategic dialogue - *fierce conversation* - between the insight professional, who knows about how the putative insight was generated, and key stakeholders who can assess the practical application of this insight. It is this strategic dialogue that will help you differentiate interesting observations from highly actionable insights capable of changing behaviour.

The Starbucks insight

We are told that the Starbucks coffee concept started with the idea of people needing a *third place*, somewhere that was between their home and their office, where they could relax and also work. One can envisage the kind of strategic dialogue that would have taken place between those who first envisioned this third place concept based on customer insight data, and the decision-makers who would need to work out exactly how this could be implemented.

The *third place insight* only becomes real when Starbucks Coffee Company stakeholders translate this concept into reality - work out exactly how this new coffee drinking experience, with sofas for people to sit, talk and access

Wi-Fi, will work in practice. It was the third place insight, in tandem with the strategic dialogue with management, that manifested Starbucks as we now know it.

Identifying a true insight involves a strategic dialogue

Asking the *So What* question will help establish if a putative insight goes beyond just being an observation and has the potential to become a viable business proposition. The better and more penetrating the questions asked about the data, the better the answers and the better the final insight and outcome.

What is the differentiating strength of your insight - its power to change behaviour?

Below are some types of question to determine what is an observation and what has the potential to be a game changing insight. The aim is to identify how likely it is that this insight will change consumer behaviour - and in precisely what way?

- Is this insight genuinely unique and differentiating?
- Is this an insight strong enough to change consumer behaviour?
- What happens when the What-If principle is applied? If this insight were introduced and applied, how would behaviour change?
- Is this insight capable of changing consumers' misconceptions about something?
- Does this insight provide an improved way of what they are currently doing?
- Does this insight provide that Aha moment for the consumer and offer a totally new solution?
- What emotional benefit does this idea provide and is there an aspirational nature to the insight?

Identifying the potential impact of an insight

Some further questions to establish whether you have a compelling insight capable of driving your storyline are reviewed below.

Will the insight create a sustainable competitive advantage?

Is this an observation that will give the organisation a competitive advantage that will help it drive growth and/or profitability? Will it make an impact on the current market dynamics?

Is it commercially viable?

Determine exactly how the insight will create revenue and profit. In short, how will money be made out of this insight? Are there metrics available to demonstrate the short-term financial benefits of, and also the longer-term commercial pay-off from, introducing this idea? In addition, establish how commercial behaviour will change as a result of introducing this insight.

Is there an organisational fit?

Another key criterion is how well the business is set up to accommodate this insight. Will this be straightforward, or will the organisational culture and outlook need to dramatically change to facilitate this insight. Related to this is just how much flexibility is built into the organisational processes and culture to accommodate this change.

Is it actionable?

Can this insight be actioned in reality? For example, just how practicable is it to identify and change the behaviour of a particular segment of customers?

Does it help futureproof the organisation?

Increasingly, organisations are looking for strategic foresights. These are fundamental trends to which it needs to respond to ensure it stays relevant and is able to cope with disruption and the changing business environment.

Does the insight have the Wow factor?

Another key criterion in establishing the power of an insight is to determine how likely it is that stakeholders will instantly and instinctively see its wow appeal. This does not guarantee that you have a genuine insight, but it helps!

Action 5: Get a sense of how your core unifying idea and insight will underpin your storyline

Build a picture in your mind of how the insight - your core unifying idea - will sit at the heart of your business solution. This is the *main thing* that will drive your evidence-based storyline. Think of this as the *North Star* that guides your journey.

How will the insight influence customer behaviour?

A good storyteller will demonstrate to stakeholders their mastery around how insights can be used to successfully drive behaviour change in the desired direction. Below we provide some perspectives that successful evidence-based storytellers are likely to focus upon when creating an insight-based narrative.

- ¤ An insight story around a *misperception* that customers may have - addressing this lies at the heart of the story.

- ¤ An insight about customer *dissatisfaction* about current solutions to a problem leads to an enhanced solution that would immediately transform customer behaviour.

- ¤ An insight that pivots around crystallising a different way of looking at the world - it opens up a hitherto unthought of *radical solution* for customers.

Virgin Atlantic vs British Airways

Let us take the example of how Virgin Atlantic might win customers from British Airways? Here there could be a mass of data about what it is that long-haul flyers like and dislike about each airline. But a compelling evidence-based storyline needs to go beyond simply building up a picture of general preferences towards each airline. This is too bland. A compelling story focuses on what is at the heart of encouraging British Airways flyers to actively switch to Virgin.

This is likely to gravitate around deep-seated perceptions around what it is to be a British Airways, as opposed to a Virgin, flyer. A compelling story will focus on the tension of the Virgin versus British Airways choice. It will look at the *dilemma* facing many travellers between enjoying the global coverage of British Airways versus the emotional pull of being part of the more radical Virgin *tribe*.

A powerful story will get a storyline going around how some people's value systems and personality will fit with the more *traditional* values of British Airways, whilst others are aligned to the more *radical* values of Virgin. Thus, unpacking the big motivational drivers will provide an engaging storyline.

Action 6: Create a visual display to support your analysis process

We would commend the merits of occasionally stepping outside the digital analysis mode and spending some time physically working with the data. Anything that gets you beyond working with software-generated charts usually helps the creative process.

Visual displayed thinking creates an engagement with the data. The act of physically writing out evidence headlines on *Post-It Notes,* and then moving these around, helps the creative process. The joy of working in this way is that it will encourage you to adopt a more integrated storytelling approach, away from data silo thinking.

We provide a practical illustration of how to do this in the Holistic Frame chapter. But in summary:

- Go through the different sources and identify the killer evidence that is beginning to emerge in answering the business question.
- Write each key piece of evidence on a separate Post-It Note.
- Physically group the Post-It Notes into groups of evidence that address a particular theme, idea or story point.
- Create a visual display by organising the Post-It Notes. This display will give you a sense of the direction of the evidence - the emerging storyline.
- Throughout the process, apply both qualitative and quantitative modes of analysis - think holistically.

FREQUENTLY ASKED QUESTIONS

Question One: Is it always possible to obtain an understanding of the big picture before getting involved in the detailed data analysis? Could there be situations where, if you did this, you fail to understand important points of detail that feed into the overall storyline?

Answer: There could be situations where you learn - via more detailed analysis - that there are two quite distinct stories within the overall top level picture. For example, the way *women* tackle health and wellbeing issues could be totally different from the way *men* tackle these issues.

So, you need to be flexible and prepared for your initial overview to change. In which case, you would then unfold these two more detailed stories. But the point is that, in the vast majority of studies, it is helpful to quickly get to the heart of what is the likely eventual overall storyline. This can be achieved in the knowledge that the subsequent detailed analysis in a high proportion of cases is only going to refine this overall storyline, rather than totally rewrite it.

Question Two: What if there is not a true (real) insight at the heart of the presentation you are about to give?

Answer: Not all investigations will unearth a true insight - something that tells us about people's motivations and guides us on how best to influence their behaviour. The reality is that some studies will simply contribute to existing contextual knowledge. In this situation, the key is signalling this research outcome in good time so that stakeholder expectations are managed.

Question Three: What is the single best way to establish whether you have a genuine insight or just an observation?

Answer: The key is to focus of whether there is a psychological *and* a behavioural dimension to the insight that provides a lever for influencing subsequent consumer behaviour.

 Top Tip

Think of your analysis as like assembling a jigsaw. To quickly get a gist of what the picture is all about, start by fitting into place the top, side and bottom edging pieces. Then follow this by fitting in a few central pieces. This is more effective than starting by fully completing just one corner of the jigsaw without having any idea of the big picture of what the jigsaw is about. In sum, start with the initial big picture before getting into the detail.

Best Next Move

Experiment to determine your own preferred style for teasing out the storyline. There is no one right method. The chosen approach should help you avoid data overwhelm and see the big picture. It should allow the integration of qualitative and quantitative data to identify key themes. And it should get to the heart of what is a genuine insight. We would commend creating a visual display using Post-It Notes to support the conventional analysis of the computer outputs, but it is a personal choice.

SUMMARY

The Strategy Frame is about first focusing on the big picture in order to avoid getting dragged down into the minutiae of the data too early in the process.

It is about quickly establishing the core storyline, but then being prepared to revise this initial view as more detailed evidence emerges.

In this frame we also stress the importance of thinking holistically - bringing the evidence together in an integrated way to unearth underlying themes. This includes recognising that there are not only qualitative and quantitative *methods* of data collection, but also qualitative and quantitative *modes* of analysing data.

Obtain total clarity around what constitutes a genuine insight. A true insight will contain two critical dimensions: a *psychological* dimension explaining people's attitudes, beliefs and feelings and a *behavioural* dimension that describes what the person is doing as a result of these causal psychological drivers.

At this early stage in the analysis process, begin to get a sense of the way your emerging insights will drive your storyline.

The key is to adopt an analysis style with which you feel comfortable. But we would recommend the use of visual displayed thinking. This fosters a creative and holistic approach in identifying the emerging storylines.

Next, we look at the *Evaluation Frame*. This puts the spotlight on assessing the robustness of your evidence against more formal methodological criteria.

4 THE EVALUATION FRAME
How to establish if your evidence is robust

The *Evaluation Frame* looks at evidence through the lens of key methodological and statistical criteria. In today's data landscape there is less emphasis on passing our evidence through the scrutiny of the more traditional methodological criteria. But we have taken the view that applying these classic criteria is a start point - a kind of touchstone - to get your detailed analysis underway.

GUIDING PRINCIPLES

Principle One: Assess the robustness of your evidence against classic research methodological criteria

There are a number of methodological criteria that provide a start point for assessing the robustness of your evidence. It is good practice to review these before looking at the data through a more pragmatic lens given what we know about how data is collected in practice.

Principle Two: Review key statistical techniques that could help you pinpoint critical insights

This is not a book on statistical analysis. But we do highlight certain key statistical concepts where the analyst should be up-to-speed in carrying out their analysis.

Principle Three: Understand how attitudes are formed , change, and relate to behaviour

There are a number of generally agreed theories/explanations of how attitudes are formed and how they relate to behaviour. It is important in interpreting the evidence to be cognisant of these fundamental tenets of attitude formation, and of the relationship of attitude to behaviour.

KEY ACTIONS

Action 1: Assess the robustness of your research design

Below we look at some specific issues of which you need to be aware in making a judgement about the robustness of the fundamental research design you are using to explore a business question.

Is this a design that provides valid and reliable measurements?

Your design should measure what it purports to measure. Any *systematic* biases that have crept into the research design could lead to questionable evidence. Let us say that the aim of a study was to examine the hypothesis that left-handed people are more creative than right-handed people. Here, unless you have carefully defined what constitutes right and left handedness, including addressing the complexity of how you define someone who is ambidextrous, then you could have invalid evidence.

Can you generalise out from this design?

We have discussed the importance of the research findings being collected in a scenario that is generalisable to the broader situation in which the decision will play itself out. For example, if you are claiming that a website is user-friendly but have only asked users to look at the website on a PC, but not on a mobile phone, then you cannot legitimately make statements about the user-friendliness of the website when accessed via a mobile phone.

Does your design provide a sufficient explanation about what is driving your key findings?

A research design must be rigorous in the sense of being able to describe why a particular relationship exists and/or provide an account of why attitudes have formed in this way. For example, it is insufficient to simply conclude that commuters do not understand a new rail tariff. There will be an expectation that the research design will explain *why* this is the case.

Action 2: Assess the technical rigor of your sampling procedures and statistically based conclusions

Below we look at some fundamental issues in assessing the robustness of data drawn from a sampling - survey - process.

Does your sample reflect the population that it purports to represent?

A key tenet of sound sampling is that the sample should reflect the population the study is intended to measure. If decisions have been taken to exclude a particular group of people from the sampling frame, then this is a major challenge to the validity of the research design. For example, if a study on the attitudes towards the UK National Health Service requires a sample of *all* individuals who are eligible to receive care under the NHS, then a sample design that excludes those over 80 years of age has shortcomings. This sampling approach does not reflect the intended population for this investigation.

Are you able to make an informed estimate of sample bias?

A further sample bias can result from individuals who are eligible for the study but who decline to take part in the survey. The critical issue here is the extent to which this non-response could bias the results.

For example, if only 5% of the population of time-urgent senior executives you want to talk to about using a new high-performance productivity app take part in your survey (because they are too busy!) , then this would represent a major bias. This level of response could mean that you are not getting feedback from the busy executives your new app is aimed at helping.

However, if your study is to determine whether a sports celebrity is an appropriate person for an organisation to sponsor, then feedback from a survey with a modest response rate could still provide a sufficiently robust *directional steer* for this decision.

Is your sample size robust enough?

- ¤ Care needs to be taken with statistics drawn from total samples below 400. These need to be interpreted with care.
- ¤ Sampling theory tells us that, if we wish to interpret a survey statistic of 50% drawn from a sample of 400, at what is referred to as the 95%

Level of Confidence, this needs to be interpreted within the range of ±5%. That is, this 50% survey statistic tells us that 95 times out of 100 the true figure is likely to fall within the range of 45-55%.

¤ If you are looking at subgroups of the population, for example those in the 18 to 24 age group, then samples of less than 100 need to be treated with particular caution.

¤ With qualitative samples, when the number of people interviewed drops below 30, then care is needed in interpreting this evidence.

Action 3: Ensure there are no fundamental methodological weaknesses in your core evidence

Let us look at some key watch-outs in understanding survey evidence and building a robust storyline.

Flawed linkages and causality

The audience will quickly lose confidence in your story if you highlight statistical correlations without being able to explain some of the causal drivers behind a relationship. You may have a statistical correlation between two variables, but if you do not have sufficient evidence to establish underlying causality, building your story around this is risky.

A related issue is the ill-informed reporting of subgroup variations. Sometimes we will see references to interest in product X being higher in region A, compared to region B. Whereas in fact, there is nothing about the region that is driving why consumers prefer product X. It could simply reflect the fact that the product is aimed at older people, and that there is a higher proportion of older people in region A compared to other regions. Avoid reporting on simple data relationships that overlook the complexity of what is driving the connection.

Substantiate your evidence

Do not build a storyline based on a piece of outlying data that is not corroborated with evidence from other research and what we already know about this topic. There is a saying that, *any figure that looks particularly interesting is probably wrong!* So always double check standout stats.

Absolute and relative movement

Surveys can struggle to provide totally accurate *absolute* readings. They are stronger in measuring *relative* change. For example, we can be confident in saying that sales of a brand of washing machine are rising if we are reporting a shift upwards from 5% to 10%. But it would be risky to take the percentage of people *claiming* they have this brand of washing machine now and from this extrapolate out to make a statement about the *actual number* in existence.

Action 4: Assess the quality of the interview process

We now provide some questions to help assess the robustness of the data collection method and the rigorousness of the questioning techniques.

Interview mode

It is well documented that the mode of an interview - whether this took place on a face-to-face basis, via the telephone or as an online survey - can substantially affect the nature of the evidence being obtained.

Engagement levels: The mode of interview can affect the level of engagement in taking part in the survey. Sometimes, for a particular situation, an online method can promote interest and engagement. But, at other times it can lower engagement (and response rates).

Openness and honesty: The presence of an interviewer in a face-to-face or telephone interview can add richness and may bring more honesty to the interviewing process. But equally the anonymity that is provided by an online interview can be an effective way of handling sensitive topics. It can produce more willingness to give information.

The level of concentration: The act of engaging with a survey in an online format could be beneficial to the survey in capturing interest. But it could be a distraction if people are dipping in and out of different emails and other calls at the same time.

Questioning techniques

It is widely recognised that the particular questioning technique used can have an impact on survey findings. Below we list some of the key questionnaire watch-outs.

The salience of the question: Questions often fail because they do not relate to the respondent's world. For example, asking in the UK: *Do you think the data protection regulations in Slovenia are sufficiently rigorous?*

The ease of comprehension: Many questions are written in technical language that may not make sense to every respondent. For example: *Was your website developed using WordPress?*

Ambiguity: Questions may contain different meanings that make it difficult for the respondent to answer. For example: *Do you agree that it should be easier for people to get onto the Council? (Get onto* can mean *become a member of* but also to *complain to*).

Leading questions: Certain questions make assumptions or lead the respondent in a particular direction. For example: *Please give me three reasons why tea is a better drink than coffee?'*

Lack of attention to wording detail: Loose inaccurate wording can make a major difference to how the question is interpreted. For example, the question, *Have you ever visited Great Britain?* (where the intention is to establish those visiting England, Scotland, Wales or Northern Ireland) fails to address the point that, although Northern Ireland is part of the *United Kingdom*, it is not part of *Great Britain*.

Ordering: The order in which statements are presented in a question can make a big difference to the outcome. For example, in a pre-coded list of brands, claimed awareness of a brand at the top will invariably be higher than if that same brand appears in the middle of the list.

There is a useful test you can apply to questionnaires. Could an ordinary person, without any specialist knowledge of this topic, answer the question? If the answer is *No* then you need to review the approach.

Action 5: Apply key attitude measurement principles

Let's look at how to measure an attitude and its relationship to behavioural change.

Be specific when measuring attitudes

You need clarity around the specific attitude you are measuring. There will be a difference between generally establishing that someone is concerned about climate change and determining that they would definitely prioritise reducing carbon emissions over economic growth.

Ensure you are measuring attitudes not platitudes

In assessing attitudes do not fall into the trap of obtaining *platitudes*: generalised clichéd off-the-shelf opinions that have been borrowed from others, and then played back as a participant's own response. The reliance on platitudes is exacerbated by the availability of *instant* comments from other people expressing their views on social media. This can trick us into thinking the attitude being expressed is actually the view of the respondent. This can lead to erroneous statements being made about what are people's true deep-seated beliefs.

The stability of attitude

Do not assume that, because an individual has been assigned to a particular attitude segment, they will *consistently* behave in this way. For example, an individual may always fly with an economy airline. But when it comes to staying in a hotel, they may be a premium buyer. For instance, they may fly easyJet to Nice, but then stay at the exclusive Negresco Hotel!

Intervening variables

In extrapolating out from current attitudes into predicting future behaviour, take into account how intervening variables can affect such predictions. Thus, someone may claim to be environmentally friendly. But in practice they may not *always* behave in this way when it actually comes to recycling (perhaps because of transport difficulties in getting to the recycling depot).

Walk the talk

We are learning to use behavioural experiments, rather than just relying on attitude measurement, to predict behaviour. Thus, individuals in a survey may *claim* to be prepared to undertake exercise each day in order to improve their health but they may not do this in practice.

One interesting example of a behavioural experiment involved offering rail travellers a free ticket if they were prepared to do ten star-jumps! This would give a measure of the propensity to take part in exercise that is based on actual behaviour - those who did the star jumps - rather than reported claimed intentions.

Action 6: Work through the fundamentals of robust qualitative evidence

There are certain factors to review in determining the robustness of qualitative evidence.

Mapping the range of attitudes

Fundamental to qualitative research is identifying - although not necessarily measuring - the range of attitudes that exist on a particular topic. It is important to ensure that qualitative research is mapping the full range of attitudes likely to surface on a particular issue.

Reflecting the variability of the target population

Qualitative research needs to be set up in such a way that those taking part reflect the variability of the population being studied. For example, if you are conducting a study amongst supporters of a football club, you need to reflect the spread of the fanbase: their age, gender, income, and region, together with frequency with which they may attend matches. Your qualitative sample needs to reflect these characteristics and behaviours.

Taking into account the moderator effect

Are the findings comparatively independent of the role played by the personality of the qualitative moderator/interviewer? We know that qualitative research is inextricably linked with the way the qualitative researcher works. So, we need reassurance that, if the study is repeated with a different moderator, it would not generate *substantially* different findings.

FREQUENTLY ASKED QUESTIONS

Question One: These days most projects are conducted in a highly pragmatic way that usually falls short of the methodological criteria used in the past -

so is there any point of applying the more fundamental methodological principles discussed in the Evaluation Frame?

> **Answer:** It remains good practice to have a clear understanding of what *classic* methodology is telling us as a start point for understanding the evidence. A great writer will be open to the latest buzzwords and phrases that young people use. But they will decide when to use these expressions based on an in-depth understanding of, and a respect for, the principles of English grammar. Relating this to insight - if you are not aware of classic best practice, and are just relying on pragmatism, this can be a slippery slope towards making unfounded interpretations.

Question Two: How do you work out whether a research study is *fit-to-purpose*?

> **Answer:** A fit-to-purpose research design is one that: provides the required level of precision; generates sufficient depth of insight; is achievable in practice; is within the acceptable budget; and can be delivered to the timetable.

Question Three: Increasingly there are no hard and fast rules about what is methodologically sound and what is less rigorous or more questionable. In this new data landscape and environment, how do I work out what is a flawed research finding and what is not?

> **Answer:** If you *smell a rat* during your analysis process you can rest assured that the audience will also tease this out on the day of the presentation. So always act on any doubts. If you do have any nagging doubts about the robustness of a piece of data, seek expert advice. Do not just assume everything will be all right on the day of the presentation.

 Top Tip

> In giving a presentation always make the assumption that there will be an expert in the audience who will test your argument to destruction against the gold standard of research theory. If you pass this methodological expert from hell test, you would be presenting from a solid platform.

Best Next Move

On your next project, identify any critical evidence that *may* be based on a methodological flaw that could undercut your overall message. Seek technical or statistical advice from an expert in order to feel totally reassured that your analysis is robust.

SUMMARY

The Evaluation Frame provides a critical touchstone against which to begin to evaluate the robustness of the evidence. It is about assessing the evidence against the research methods *gold standard:* what we know from traditional statistics and research methodology.

Passing your evidence through the lens of more traditional evaluation criteria provides a robust starting point for your analysis. Check for validity, reliability and generalisability.

There are a number of critical watch-outs. First, make sure your sample reflects the population you are researching. Also check the level of non-response: are you getting sufficient feedback from the people to whom you should be talking?

Be alert to any critical flaws in the interviewing and questionnaire design process that could jeopardise the robustness of your conclusions.

Ensure the interviewing process is professional and robust. Ensure you are not measuring general clichéd platitudes but are getting to the heart of peoples' true attitudes.

Ensure those recruited into the qualitative research reflects the range of attitudes in play on the topic being investigated.

Next we look at the *Experience Frame*. We examine the evidence from the perspective of the practical experience gained in conducting research.

5 THE EXPERIENCE FRAME
How to apply your judgement to the analysis

The *Experience Frame* is about applying practical knowledge that has been built up over the years about how different research techniques actually work in practice. An understanding of commercial research practice needs to be factored into our analysis, alongside more formal methodological criteria.

GUIDING PRINCIPLES

Principle One: The mind of the customer insight professional is admissible evidence

Apply your own experience and judgement of what has worked well in the past. This can be used to interpret and enhance the analysis. Be confident in applying this knowledge.

Principle Two: Apply the Panorama Principle - context explains everything!

Understand the wider context to the way your evidence was collected. It is important to be aware of everything that was going on around the project while it was being conducted.

Principle Three: Interpret the evidence against available norms, benchmarks and best practice guidelines

Over the years, the industry has generated a body of empirical evidence - including various norms and benchmarks - that help us interpret the data. Apply this comparative and contextual knowledge to enhance the quality of the analysis.

KEY ACTIONS

Action 1: Interpret your evidence based on an informed appraisal of how sampling really works

We now explore some practical sampling considerations of which it is important to be aware - how everyday commercial practice works.

How the sample selection process works in practice

We need to be alert to where there could be practices at work within the sampling process that lead us to survey respondents who may not fully reflect the population we intend to research.

Self-selection

One issue is that individuals can be routed to different online surveys where they can select whether they take part or not and, if not, they will be offered up an alternative survey. This introduces a systematic bias that is difficult to measure. Sometimes this is not going to be an issue, but sometimes it could be. You need to be alert to this issue - ask the sample provider to explain the precise steps in their sampling process.

Incentivised respondents

Another issue is the impact of offering incentives to participants - respondents. You want to ensure that you do not have a sample of, what we may term, *professional* respondents who do not reflect the wider population? When incentives are being offered for taking part in a survey you need to check that individuals cannot second guess, at the qualification stage, what category of person is needed to take part in the survey. An example here would be a respondent, who in order to secure the incentive, claims to be a BMW owner whereas in fact they drive a Ford.

Token responses

Some respondents participating in online surveys may be *speedsters*, that is completing the survey so quickly that they are unlikely to have taken the interview seriously. There is also the related issue of *flatliners* - individuals who give the same answer on a rating scale, across a number of questions. This can be going for the top position, the bottom position, or always picking the midpoint for each question. This suggests they are not taking the survey seriously. Agencies will help you identify professional respondents, speedsters, and flatliners, and eliminate them from your sample.

Hard to find samples

If the definition of the target audience becomes too onerous and restrictive, this can lead to an interviewer pushing the boundaries of acceptability in terms of the individuals they allow into the sample. For example, if the requirement is for an individual to currently own a Ferrari, and also to have owned a Mercedes in the last three years, this in itself is quite a demanding requirement. But, if we added a third requirement, such as they must have attended a Formula One racing event in the last year, then we are inviting difficulties!

Talking to the right person

Given time and budget pressures with certain commercial market research projects, compromises are made in terms of deciding on the person with whom we should be speaking about this topic.

Joint household decision-making

Let us take the example of a study aimed at understanding the extent to which families understand finance and have debt under control. The easy route here is to conduct a survey with the *person who is most responsible for making financial decisions*. And there will be households where there is a *head of household*, who is the dominant and sole decision-maker on all things financial.

But there will be a substantial proportion of households where finances are dealt with on a *joint basis*, with a partner or a spouse taking joint responsibility. In these joint financial decision-making situations, an interview with one person will gloss over the complexities. There will be gaps in our understanding of debt management by opting for the convenient route of speaking to the person who mostly, but not exclusively, looks after the family's household finances.

Business decision-making units

Another example would be from the world of business-to-business research, where a complex decision-making unit will make decisions about buying a particular piece of equipment. But you will find many business-to-business research studies that, in order to save time and money, try to cut through this by asking to speak to the *person most responsible for purchasing a piece of equipment* or the person who has the *greatest influence on purchasing this equipment*. This can lead to a very simplistic understanding of the issue.

Pin down the extent of any response bias

Commercial research ultimately is about coming up with a fit-to-purpose design. In certain situations, the fact that a piece of research has comparatively low levels of response will not dramatically interfere with the way the business question is addressed. But there will be many situations where a lack of clarity around the level of sample bias and non-response bias will be a major issue. One of the problems is that different fieldwork agencies could be using a variety of terms to explain the nature and extent of these biases.

Response rate

At one end of the spectrum, there could be an agency that is reporting a *response rate* on a survey that meets the classic definition of what this term means when using probability-based sampling. (This will provide precise details on those who were eligible for the study, those who were successfully contacted, those who refused, and those who took part.)

Strike rate

At the other end of the spectrum, a different agency may use various terms such as *strike rate* or *hit rate* to give an indication of how many people were contacted to arrive at the final achieved sample. This strike rate may not provide details of those who were not eligible to take part in the survey, those who refused, and so on. Having this information may not always be important. But, in certain scenarios, *not* having the data about exactly how the final sample was arrived at will be critical. You need to check this out.

Be clear on the representativeness of your sample

If you were building a storyline about people's attitudes towards installing solar panel heating based on a sample of 400 homeowners, you need to know whether this is a representative sample or skewed towards those who are more environmentally friendly. So, if in order to generate this sample of 400, over 4,000 people were contacted, you would need to be told this, together with the status of the 3,600 who did not take part.

Did the non-respondents *not qualify* as homeowners or was it that they *refused* to take part in the study because they are not interested in environmental issues? Knowing this is central to your storyline about the level of interest in solar panel heating.

The key point here is that, on certain issues, the level of response is not a critical interpretation factor, but in other situations it could be vital to determining the robustness of your storyline.

Quality control

With regard to really understanding what is going on with your sample, first make sure you are aware of the effectiveness of the quality control checks that the fieldwork company will build in to minimise the chances of professional respondents second guessing what the topic is about and self-selecting themselves into a survey. In addition, for online sample panels there is an ESOMAR guideline which provides a series of questions to ask about how an online sample has been constructed. This will give you a good indication of the quality of the sample with which you are working.

Action 2: Apply caution when interpreting sample error estimates

It is important not to assume that the textbook formulae for calculating sampling error tells the full story. It pays to err on the side of caution. This is because the conditions underpinning this *theoretical* sampling error calculation are rarely met in practice. There is a body of empirical knowledge about the sampling process that tells us that (as a minimum) you may need to double this estimate to be certain that you have a significant finding!

This takes us into the complex territory of calculating the *design effect* - on which you should seek expert statistical advice. The design effect principle recognises that it is rarely possible to meet the underlying assumptions behind the textbook sampling error formula and allows us to arrive at a more realistic estimate.

Test for statistical significance <u>and</u> common sense

¤ There are various statistical tests that can be applied to establish whether or not the difference between the two sample statistics is significant - that is, it goes beyond what might be expected from random variations in the sample data.

¤ However, in identifying what is a robust finding on which to take action, it is important to combine tests of statistical significance with common sense checks. Make sure a statistical observation squares with what is already known about a topic and makes sense in business terms.

Action 3: Ensure you have an informed view of how professional interviewing works in practice

There are a number of practical issues about the interviewing and questioning process to explore to be sure your storyline is being built on a sound evidence-based platform. Below we provide some watch-outs:

Has the interview been set up as an engaging dialogue, <u>not</u> just as a checklist of unrelated questions?

There is a massive difference between a checklist of unrelated questions - where the respondent is expected to answer in a robotic way - and a well-structured *dialogue*. The former leads to speedster respondents who will rattle through the survey questions without giving them much thought or care. A dialogue is more likely to elicit robust responses.

Look out for any lack of precision

Clearly, accurately defining key words and terms is critically important. For instance, asking someone whether they own a car or not might seem simple. But there are lots of complications around whether a person *owns* or is *leasing* the car, or has *regular use* of someone else's car, and a host of other factors.

Watch out for improvisation!

When a questionnaire is poorly designed, the interviewer and the respondent may sometimes, for the best of intentions, try to make the questionnaire work. Thus, a summary of the transcript of such a flawed interview could be something like this:

Interviewer: Do you own a car?

Respondent: I don't own a car, but I use my son's car and drive it regularly, so shall we say I sort of own a car, and say yes to that question?

Interviewer: I guess that will be all right. Let's now come onto the questions about how you decided what brand of car to buy!

You get the idea! Given the lack of clarity around defining exactly what is meant by car ownership, the interviewer and respondent will between themselves attempt to make a flawed questionnaire work. It is very difficult to identify this in the data outputs. But if alarm bells are ringing at the data analysis stage, you need to need to go back and revisit how critical terms used in the questionnaire were defined.

The impact of social media – understand the context

Be aware of how - in today's social media environment - attitudes may swing more dramatically than they have done in the past. Attitudes are made up of our own beliefs and knowledge about a particular phenomenon, coupled with our perceptions of what we think other people think about our attitude. This *social cognition* process is well understood. But what has changed is the way that people now have instantaneous, widespread access, via social media, to so many different points of view. This can be very influential in shaping the way they think. This can lead to quite dramatic swings in the way attitudes are formed and changed.

For example, via the *#meToo* movement, women can now gain widespread and instantaneous access to how other women feel about the way they are treated in the workplace. In a short space of time, this sharing has radically transformed thinking about what is acceptable and unacceptable behaviour.

Be clear on how to interpret evidence from questions that have been gamified

In order to encourage people to respond to surveys these days, certain questions may be turned into a game (*gamified*) to make them more interesting and engaging. On balance, this is to be commended. But the analyst needs to be aware of where the change in the context for the question to make it more engaging - to gamify it - may introduce a subtle change to the way the question is interpreted, and then answered, by the respondent. Here we provide some illustrative examples.

What is your favourite meal?

If the aim of a study is to find out the favourite meal of the typical French person, then to make this question more interesting, the gamified version, might be: *'Imagine you were about to eat your last meal before going to the guillotine in the French Revolution, what meal would you most like to eat?'* However, the big build-up to this - the question setup - may encourage French people to showcase Cordon Bleu, haute cuisine or classic French dishes. Whereas, in fact, we are fairly sure that the favourite meal of the French is simple steak and frites!

If you were the Director General of the BBC...

Another example would be gamifying the process of identifying what TV programmes people would most like to view. This could be achieved by casting the respondent in the *role* of the Director General of the BBC. This could however bias the respondent to giving responses that reflected the BBC's remit to *inform, educate and entertain.* This could lead to a very earnest listing of programmes, including erudite documentaries on worthy subjects such as climate change. Whereas this particular respondent may not in fact personally like any of these more worthy programmes and would prefer to see more soap operas, reality TV and celebrity ten-pin bowling!

Action 4: Make use of norms and benchmarks

It is important to seek out from industry sources and/or client organisations, norms and benchmarks that will help you interpret the evidence. Below we look at some categories where norms are available.

Question response norms

There is a body of knowledge about how certain *research effects* work. For example, we have mentioned the example of recall of a brand being higher if this brand is at the top, rather than the middle of bottom, of a list. Another illustration is that when familiar names, such as IBM or Microsoft, are added to the list of options in a questionnaire on IT suppliers, then these big names tend to be cited - even if they do not even make the product in question! This has led to the insight industry building up an understanding of how to *adjust* for inflated, overstated or understated responses.

Politeness bias

Another issue is interpreting findings in light of cultural and language factors. Care needs to be taken in comparing results from one country to another. We know that there is a politeness bias at work in many Asian and Middle Eastern countries. There will be a reluctance to criticise, or be dissatisfied with a product, out of a concern about offending. In addition, we know that the way individuals use word scales will vary by country. In some countries, there is a tendency for respondents to only use the top end of the scale, whereas in other countries they favour using the lower end of the scale.

Question rating scales

It is important to take into account what *norms* have been built up using particular question rating scales. For example, FMCG companies often use a carefully validated seven-point scale to measure the likelihood of purchasing a brand. These will be assessed against norms about what actually happened when applying these scales in the marketplace over the years. This leads to observations such as around one third of those who opted for the top box (the *definitely would buy* point on the scale) would in practice at least try the product in a real-life market situation. These norms will be sector and company specific. So, you need to talk to colleagues in order to identify the best source of normative data to help with interpreting the evidence.

Action 5: Know how to interpret qualitative research outputs

Below we identify some key practical watch-outs to ensure you are building a story around qualitative evidence that is robust.

The recruitment process

Many qualitative research participants are often drawn from a previously recruited *panel* of individuals who have agreed to take part in qualitative research studies. This can be a pragmatic and sensible way of undertaking research within reasonable cost parameters. But you need to be alert to respondents who have taken part in a series of focus groups or interviews in a particular product category, and therefore may *not* be providing a typical range of attitudes.

The quality of the depth interviewer/moderator interventions

Around the world there will be a massively wide variation in the quality and experience of qualitative research moderators. Inexperience in qualitative research may manifest itself in different ways. Some qualitative researchers may bring too many of their own personal viewpoints into the research process. They may not always have the conceptual skill to stand back and look more objectively at the key constructs in play.

Some moderators, who are not operating from any psychological platform, could therefore be naively using, for example, different *projective* and *enabling techniques* that more experienced moderators know only work with certain personality types.

The way the analysis was conducted

We have stressed the importance of qualitative research being analysed both in qualitative and quantitative modes. This though requires a rigorous process for recording what happened in the group or depth interview. But if the group or interview did not allow for proper note-taking or transcription, then the subsequent analysis could be based on only impressionistic top line recollections, rather than a more detailed content analysis.

Action 6: Be aware of the major pitfalls in interpreting secondary data sources

Below we highlight some issues that the experienced analyst will take into account in interpreting secondary evidence to help advance their robust storyline.

The sponsorship of research

The fact that an organisation has sponsored or funded a particular study does not automatically mean that the evidence will be biased in a particular direction. But clearly this is a key watch-out. For example, an organisation that has aligned itself with being sceptical about global warming may be selective in its use of the scientific evidence on this topic.

The way the research evidence is framed

Subtle biases can creep into the reporting of data simply through the way a statistic is framed or primed. A notorious illustration of framing comes from the OJ Simpson trial, where the defence lawyers continually repeated the *assertion* that only around 1 in 1,000 abused women are murdered by their husband. A wider framing could have been that of wives who were murdered, who had been subject to proven domestic violence from their husband (the situation in the OJ Simpson case) then, in 8 in 10 of these cases, the murder was committed by the husband!

Identifying what is really driving a conclusion

It is important to understand what is underpinning a research-based conclusion. One example is the interpretation of performance league tables. The criteria used to create these league table rankings will be critical. For instance, let's say a particular town emerges as *the best place to live in the country*. Is this true or does it reflect the weighting given to the criteria used to create this league table?

This top billing could be based on the town having high scores on certain fairly arbitrarily determined criteria which carried a high weighting in the assessment. These could be, *having excellent childcare* and *good medical facilities*. However, if other criteria with different weightings had been applied, such as *a good local transport network* and *first-class entertainment facilities*, then a different town could have been in the top spot.

FREQUENTLY ASKED QUESTIONS

Question One: If you are a newcomer to customer insight, what is the best way to get that extra depth of understanding about how the research process works in practice?

> **Answer:** Customer insight is essentially a practice-led, not theory-led, discipline. So, it is always worth assuming that there *is* existing practical knowledge and knowhow available around the issue under investigation. A good start point for checking out what we know about how research methods work in practice is to talk to a senior colleague. Then follow this

up by checking out some of the points and reference sources they may mention.

Question Two: Are the norms and benchmarks needed to interpret survey findings always readily available?

Answer: A lot of norms will be commercially sensitive in the sense that they are being built up by companies to interpret their own data. A lot of it comes down to your level of curiosity, tenacity and forensic energy in talking to colleagues, and following up leads. Work hard to make sure you have accessed what is available in the public domain.

Question Three: Just how far can you go in interrogating a research agency or online panel provider about exactly how they may have departed from a more *classic* methodological approach in order to provide a cost-effective and timely solution?

Answer: Most agencies will be pleased to answer your questions. Research is ultimately a trade-off of the following factors: the need for precision; the depth of understanding required; the available budget; the time allowed for the study; and the need to overcome practical challenges. Most agencies will attempt to arrive at the best possible trade-off. So, it is a matter of having a sensible dialogue about whether the agency has arrived at a fit-to-purpose design.

 Top Tip

Cultivate a *sixth sense* for identifying any aspect of your research process that, if flawed or in error, could undermine your analysis and conclusions. Develop an instinct for teasing out any factors in the way the research was conducted that could destroy the integrity of your core message.

 Best Next Move

On your next project, identify the critical pieces of evidence that underpin your conclusion. Ensure this evidence is not based on a research technique that has not been tried and tested. If you have any concerns about this, then pinpoint the action you are going to take to find out - from expert sources - exactly how this research technique works - and take any remedial action.

SUMMARY

The *Experience Frame* is about factoring into the analysis an understanding of how customer insight research really works in everyday practice. There is often a need to depart from the gold standard of ideal best practice.

It is important to establish whether the evidence squares with prior knowledge and is consistent with what we know about how the research techniques employed actually work in practice.

Think about the trustworthiness of the evidence. Is there anything that could have dramatically skewed the evidence in a particular direction - anything that could be responsible for a particularly *interesting* or *stand-out* finding?

With regard to interpreting sample survey statistics, apply caution to what the textbooks are telling you about the margin of error within which to interpret survey statistics.

Apply available empirical norms and other benchmarks to make sense of the evidence.

Be clear on the influence the moderator/interviewer may have had on the qualitative research process.

Look out for any bias in the framing of secondary evidence.

Next, we look at the *Enrichment Frame*. This acknowledges that it is legitimate for experienced insight researchers - within boundaries - to enhance and enrich the evidence in order to build their storyline.

THE ENRICHMENT FRAME
How to apply creativity to your analysis

The *Enrichment Frame* looks at opportunities to enrich the analysis of the data. We look at the notion of *compensating* for any shortfalls in the evidence. We also look at creative techniques to extend our understanding of the evidence.

GUIDING PRINCIPLES

Principle One: Apply the Compensation Concept

The process of compensation is about identifying any limitation in the data and using contextual knowledge to flesh out the full meaning of the data. This is *not* about changing the fundamental meaning of a piece of evidence or statistic but enhancing it.

Principle Two: Use enabling techniques to enrich the evidence

Today, it is legitimate for the customer insight professional to add their own experience and knowledge. They are *admissible evidence.* They need to liberate themselves from the straitjacket of *the literal* data. They are well placed to apply their expertise to turn bland data into a richer, more comprehensive account. It is helpful to think of the research process as initially providing us with a black and white picture. But then, through the enabling role, this is turned into living colour by drawing on related evidence and applying informed intuition.

Principle Three: Make the consultative leap to bridge the data-decision gap

Be confident in bridging the data-decision gap. In the past the customer insight professional may have been discouraged from playing this consultative role offering a point of view. This could be considered as lacking objectivity. But, harnessing an insight professional's consultative experience, alongside the evidence, is now welcomed.

KEY ACTIONS

Action 1: Compensate for methodological limitations

It is helpful to think of data as needing some form of compensation. This is about the intelligent *embellishment* of the original data. It is rare to have the ideal evidence platform for decision-making. There will often be aspects of the survey process that are less than perfect or optimum. However, in many scenarios it is possible, through sensible compensation, to still use the available evidence. This is achieved by applying common sense, intuition and experience to the core data.

Let's say you are undertaking a project for a coffee house chain where, midway through your customer satisfaction survey, there was a media-storm around the adequacy of the labelling of the chain's product ingredients. Here you might want to compensate by setting the customer satisfaction scores in the context of a wider set of readings taken over the last year.

Clearly there could be fundamental flaws in a dataset for which it is *not* possible to provide any compensation. For example, if you should have interviewed people living in small villages, and the sample ended up being massively skewed towards major cities, it could be difficult to compensate and adjust for this.

Action 2: Add colour and depth to the black and white data

It is entirely legitimate for the analyst to use their experience and judgement, within certain boundaries, to enhance their interpretation of the evidence by using different enabling techniques.

Enrich your primary evidence with supporting secondary data

Survey analysts can become so preoccupied with their own survey data that they do not take the extra step to examine this alongside powerful contextualising evidence. Let's take the example of a project on the challenges faced by start-up businesses in the UK. With such a project, there is no excuse for not setting the survey findings in the context of powerful body of evidence about UK start-ups.

Build embellished personas by making reasonable assumptions about their behaviour

In order to paint a vivid picture of an archetypal customer from a particular market segment, why not build a rounded *persona* of this type of customer? Apply some artistic license in the spirit of painting a memorable picture for the audience. Construct a *day in the life* account of their behaviour to give a sense of the way they see the world.

This may involve creating small details of this personas' life to help build a compelling account of the archetype. Let's take the example of painting a *pen portrait* of a particular banking customer archetype. We could take the audience through a typical day in their life, starting with them going for morning coffee. But, as we do not know whether they go to Costa or Starbucks, it is legitimate to embellish this *day in the life* story by making informed judgements - based on best available evidence - about where this archetype segment is most likely to take their coffee.

This is not the slippery slope to the world of alternative facts and a *anything goes with data* culture. Everything you do must be totally accountable and transparent. What you are doing is to make it easier for the audience to engage with your insight and take action.

Semiotic analysis - going deeper with the interpretation

Semiotics help us better understand what is going on under the surface by understanding the codes and symbols in play. It helps explore the context around an observation and go beyond the literal data. Semiotics provides us with rich insights about how people see the world. For example, we may have *facts* about the excellent performance of the Porsche *car*, and information about their *owners*. But a semiotician would be able to unpack the reasons why the words *Porsche driver* often evokes a certain reaction. Perhaps unjustifiably, this phrase has become associated with conspicuously wealthy and somewhat flashy personalities.

Action 3: Contribute your sector knowledge to enrich your interpretation

Market research practitioners should be prepared to bring the richness of their own experience of a business sector in helping to create a more informed interpretation. Over the years they will have built up a set of business *heuristics* (rules of thumb for fast and informed decision-making) about what does and does not work in different sectors.

For example, let's say you have undertaken extensive research on behalf of a business publisher working on a range of magazines. There will be knowledge on how different design formats work with readers. You should be encouraged to share these established principles about how readers react to different layouts.

For instance, we know that, when looking at a page of any magazine, people generally look at the top right-hand corner before the bottom left-hand corner. Given this there is no reason to believe this general principle - learnt from working across different sectors - will not apply to the specific magazine in question.

Action 4: Reframe the evidence to touch your audience's world

The experienced insight consultant will use business frameworks and heuristics that reflect the way stakeholders make sense of what's going on. Specifically, insight professionals will reframe the evidence to tap into the way their audience sees the world.

Consultants often use simple frameworks and matrices in order to illustrate key points. They know that stakeholders find these helpful in quickly absorbing information.

The Ansoff Matrix example

Let's take the example of a study conducted on behalf of a wealthy business mogul who is about to purchase a UK Premiership football club. He needs an analysis of the opportunities to maximise his investment. Here you start getting insights around:

- Selling more season tickets to existing fans.
- Setting up a women's team.

¤ Extending the season ticket offer to include different dining options at the club restaurant.

¤ Leasing the stadium to a US National Football League team who could then play some of their matches in the UK.

With this wide variety of options, a helpful business framework to communicate these ideas is the classic *Ansoff Matrix*. Below we illustrate what this might look like. This framework will be familiar to many senior decision-makers and therefore an excellent way of showcasing your insights.

The Ansoff Matrix: a Premiership Football Club acquisition

	Current product	New product
Current market	*Market Penetration* Selling more season tickets to existing fans	*Product Development* Expand season ticket offer to include dining options at club restaurant
New market	*Market Development* Setting up a women's team	*Diversification* Using stadium for NFL matches

Telling the customer story

A further way of *reframing* the evidence is to tell the story through the eyes of an individual customer. For example, if you are telling the story of a typical grocery outlet customer, why not go beyond presenting aggregate statistics - how much they spend on a typical shop and what they liked and disliked about the experience, and so on. Instead, bring this alive. You could reframe these aggregate statistics and tell the story of *a day in the life of Sally* - a typical customer of the grocery store.

By personalising the data - reframing it - around a modal customer we can bring the story alive. Instead of having tedious data tables on *likes* and *dislikes*, we could tell Sally's story. If she were *CEO for the day*, what would she change in the store? You could also have illustrations of the *Tweets* Sally might send about her experience of being in charge of the store for a day.

Action 5: Apply informed intuition and consultative judgement to your analysis

Today, the insight professional is expected to bring their own experience to bear in interpreting the evidence. They should draw on their intuition in an *informed* way.

The notion of intuition - knowing without knowing why

Intuition is powerful because it is often based on organised and deep reflection. It is not some whimsical spur of the moment thought process but can be based on profound contemplative thinking about an issue.

Intuition works implicitly through the brain's ability to discover underlying shapes and patterns that explain what has and has not worked well in the past. This helps to constantly refine the quality of our intuitive thought processes.

Intuition reflects the way that we often pick up things by osmosis, not necessarily via explicit knowledge. Intuitive analysis is a powerful way of interpreting ambiguity and translating implicit knowledge into practical knowhow.

Let's review the upside and downside of intuitive judgement.

Intuition can be our friend because:
- It is based on deep, organised reflection.
- It can be cultivated: practice helps.
- It helps to make sense of with ambiguity, uncertainty and imperfection.
- It involves flexible, circular - not just rigid and linear thinking.
- It involves both slow, gradual thinking <u>and</u> fast, instant conceptual leaps.
- It usually has a practical, as opposed to theoretical, knowledge base (knowing instinctively how to do something helps).
- It combines classic <u>and</u> emotional intelligence.

Intuition can be a false friend - it can be plain wrong. . .
- Common sense intuition can be wrong. For instance, most people would not pick 1 2 3 4 5 6 as their lottery ticket numbers. But the

probability of this combination of winning the lottery is exactly the same as any other combination of six numbers.

¤ Our memory plays tricks and we can forget the failure of our past intuitive judgements.

¤ Intellectual laziness - people default to instant intuitive thought where they would have been better investing in reflective - albeit more time-consuming - careful reasoning.

¤ A macho decision style can evolve whereby instant judgement is always seen as being better than following a more systematic reasoning process.

¤ Cognitive biases can weaken the power of spontaneous intuitive judgements. For example, we know that, when a solution is framed in the form of positive gains, this will often be chosen over the exact same solution framed in a negative way - highlighting the losses.

The sweet spot: informed intuition

It is important to play to the strengths of our intuition whilst being alert to the possible dangers. Remember that *the data may be dumb, but beliefs may be blind*. We need to find the sweet spot - informed intuition. It is about finding the balance between what the hard evidence is telling us and how we can enrich this by playing to our intuitive thinking.

It is helpful to think of decisions being based on a mixture of data and intuition. Let's take the example of Mercedes manufactured *Smart Car* where there was insufficient space for a spare wheel. There was an initial intuitive creative leap: did the Smart Car even need a spare wheel? Why not just provide an instant tyre repair kit.

However, the final decision was not *just* made based on an intuitive spark of creative thinking. It was also based on solid survey feedback that confirmed the acceptability and practicality of this solution. This is a classic example of combined intuitive and data-based decision-making.

Action 6: Identify strategic foresights and futureproof the organisation

Increasingly the customer insight professional is expected to enrich the analysis process by separating out *fads* from strategic foresights - robust and substantial trends that point to a change in customer thinking.

One definition of strategic foresight:

> *Building business advantage with an informed and credible perspective on peoples' future wants, needs or beliefs resulting from synergies amongst trends that have a practical application.*

The creation of a strategic foresight starts with *data points*. These are then grouped to form an *observation*. These observations are then assembled to identify major *themes*. This leads to the identification of *trend*. Trends can then be brought together to identify a key *strategic foresight*. This is a statement about current and likely future events, to which a business needs to respond to remain competitive. Strategic foresights lie at the core of *futureproofing* the organisation.

FREQUENTLY ASKED QUESTIONS

Question One: What are the ground rules around the process of *enriching the evidence?*

> **Answer:** Anything you do to enrich the data or compensate for any gaps should be premised on professional judgement and integrity and be made totally transparent to stakeholders.

Question Two: What is the exact process for communicating to stakeholders where the data has been enriched and where it is literal evidence from the primary qualitative or quantitative evidence?

> **Answer:** Make it clear to the audience where you have: an *actual statistic;* where you have an *estimate;* where you have a *projection;* and where there is an *embellishment* or *enrichment* of a point. You do not want the audience to go away with the false impression about the status of a piece of evidence, i.e. with ambiguity about whether it is a factual observation, or

an evidence-based judgement. Look closely at how you will preface and introduce each point, so no misreporting takes place.

Question Three: With regard to bridging the data-decision gap and making the consultative leap, exactly how far can the analyst go in providing their own point of view?

Answer: The insight professional should express their point of view. It is legitimate to add relevant experience and contextual knowledge to provide an extra dimension to the analysis. However, this is *not* an invitation to express a personal unsubstantiated viewpoint.

 Top Tip

Put some of yourself into the presentation - develop the confidence to enrich the data to bring it alive. Go beyond the literal data by painting a picture of how this insight could open up opportunities for the organisation. Do not just turn up for a presentation and hide behind an array of numbers. But you need to do this with integrity and transparency.

 Best Next Move

On your next project identify elements of your emerging storyline where your audience would benefit from you enriching the analysis to bring a critical issue alive. Apply the compensation principle: add wider context and/or greater depth by drawing on available related data sources. Make sure you explain this process in a transparent way.

SUMMARY

The Enrichment Frame is about giving the insight professional the belief and confidence in taking the extra step to enhance the data - bring it alive in the spirit of improving the decision-making process.

It is legitimate to enhance the stakeholders' understanding of the literal survey data by intelligently *compensating* for any gaps by using relevant contextual evidence.

There is a wide variety of contextual evidence to help strengthen, reframe and bring alive the primary research evidence that has been collected to answer the business question.

We have established that the mind of the customer insight professional is now acknowledged as *admissible evidence.* Their knowledge of what has worked in the past can sit alongside the primary customer insight evidence. Using relevant business heuristics and frameworks will help.

It is about arriving at the sweet spot of informed intuition where the data is contextualised in terms of the consultant's own world view and experience.

The ultimate enrichment is arguably the ability to combine the data with an understanding of other wider trends in order to identify *strategic foresights* to help futureproof the organisation.

Next, we look at the *Holistic Frame* - the final of our Seven Frames. This provides an analysis framework for integrating the evidence that will underpin your storyline.

7 THE HOLISTIC FRAME
How to build the holistic picture

The *Holistic Frame* provides you with concepts and principles - almost a new language - that allows you to present an integrated narrative, rather than simply present isolated disjointed pieces of data.

GUIDING PRINCIPLES

Principle One: Think like a holistic sensemaker not just a statistician

Statistical significance only takes us so far. The data also needs to be substantive: it needs to be *relevant* to the business problem and make sense with what we know intuitively. This takes us to the value of sensemaking: using holistic analysis techniques to build the story.

Principle Two: Frame the decision choices

Former IBM Chairman, Lou Gerstner said, *'Decision-making is easy once someone has framed the decision choices for me!'* The role of the customer insight professional is to frame the decision choices for the audience and to help to facilitate the optimum decision. Start by identifying a finite number of (prioritised) decision choices - together with supporting evidence - and take decision-makers through a process for evaluating the options.

Principle Three: Use holistic analysis concepts to integrate your evidence

Holistic analysis concepts help us make sense of multiple, often imperfect, data sources and facilitate the creation of an integrated *attacking* narrative. Holistic concepts also help to avoid the trap of presenting silos of data based on the research process, rather than answering the business question. It is also important to explain your storyline with user-friendly holistic analysis *language*.

KEY ACTIONS

Action 1: Frame the decision choices open to the decision-maker

The high performance customer insight professional will frame the decision choices, following a process whereby the merits of the decision choices are closely evaluated before arriving at a final recommendation.

The benefits of the framing approach

Framing of decision choices has the benefit of taking dysfunctionality out of the decision-making process that can exist within an organisation. It helps reduce the chances of stakeholders taking a partisan position that is not related to the evidence.

This approach avoids the insight professional getting boxed into the corner of having to *sell* a particular decision or outcome to stakeholders who are clamouring for a recommendation.

This can create a unidimensional *what's your recommendation?* culture that pivots around persuading stakeholders to a point of view in a hostile environment. This can create dysfunctionality because it becomes about *selling* a plan to stakeholders, rather than an informed evaluation of the decision options. Framing the decision choices is the more productive route.

Avoiding the Just Give Me the Answer syndrome

The decision framing approach avoids the danger of the insight professional being pressured into selecting *one* decision option that they then have to slavishly defend. This limits their flexibility for reviewing a selection of viable options. It avoids a macho *get to the point/what is your recommendation?* situation.

From the insight agency standpoint, the framing of decision choices approach lessens the chances of them being treated as a *vendor* who is just supplying (commoditised) tactical data.

Framing the choices pushes up the probability of an agency being positioned as a *trusted insight advisor,* helping to review decision options and drive the growth and change agenda.

Action 2: Apply the notion of evidence having Weight, Power and Direction

Below we share a holistic analysis framework - a *mental model* - that will help the insight professional draw together evidence from different qualitative, quantitative and big data sources into an integrated whole. The concept of evidence having *weight, power* and *direction* helps you create an integrated story and discourages the presentation of blocks of loosely related data.

Weight of Evidence

The weight of evidence includes a measure of the overall *quantitative* balance of support on a particular issue. This concept also includes examining the *qualitative* depth of feeling expressed on this issue: just how emotionally intense is this level of support?

Working with these two constructs - the quantity of support and qualitative depth of feeling - we can set up a 2X2 matrix that produces the four categories shown below.

Compelling evidence: When we have high *numerical support* for a particular event, coupled with a strong (high) *depth of feeling* being expressed, we have evidence that is *compelling.*

Watching brief evidence: This is where there is low *numerical support* for an issue, but where those who do cite this do so with *high intensity* (depth of feeling). Here we need to keep a *watching brief* on whether this evidence could be telling us something important.

Contextual evidence: This is where we have high *numerical support,* but with comparatively low *depth of feeling.* Here we need to acknowledge the quantitative levels of support and treat this as an affirmation of interest in this issue, albeit without much emotional commitment - it is *contextual evidence.*

Low priority evidence: When there is limited *numerical support* for a particular idea, and there is a low *level of engagement* of (depth of feeling) being expressed, we have *low priority* evidence.

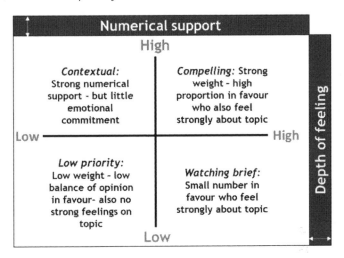

Power of Evidence

This looks at the robustness of a piece of evidence from two perspectives. Specifically, it allows us to examine the evidence through the lens of methodological theory - the Evaluation Frame. It does this in conjunction with what the practical Experience Frame is telling us about robustness. This type of analysis produces the following categories of evidence:

Solid evidence: This type of evidence meets the classic evaluation theory we identified in the Evaluation Frame. At the same time this evidence meets the experienced-based robustness criterion outlined in the Experience Frame.

Apply pragmatism: This evidence is robust in the sense that it squares with what we know from our practical experience of what works. But there remain question marks about its robustness when assessed against formal methodological criteria. So, take this evidence into account when building the story, but exercise caution.

Check practicability: This evidence meets much of the formal criteria referred to in the Evaluation Frame. But there are concerns about how this method works in everyday commercial practice.

Unsafe evidence: This is evidence that is not robust either from a methodological nor practical standpoint. Clearly this type of evidence is very questionable and can be classified as unsafe to use in building your story.

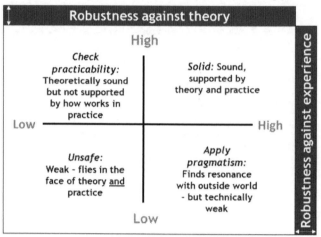

Direction of Evidence

This concept allows us to examine the evidence emerging around a particular issue from two perspectives. There is the *internal consistency* of a particular category of evidence you are using to support your storyline. And there is the *external consistency* of this overall category of evidence with other categories of evidence.

> **Internal consistency:** This refers to whether there is a high or low consistency *within* the datasets that make up this category of evidence. Is it a consistently strong, or rather fragmented and patchy picture? For example, if we have conducted 12 focus groups on a topic, are all the focus groups broadly telling a similar story, or is there massive variation in what went on across the different focus groups?

> **External consistency:** This focuses on whether the available evidence on the topic drawn from different categories of research essentially points in the same direction or not. Do we have a pattern of results that holds true *across* the qualitative, quantitative and other types of insight research used during the project? Or, is the conclusion based on a much more fragmented picture?

Working with these constructs we can identify the following scenarios:

Directionally sound indicator: This is evidence that is both internally and externally consistent.

Internally consistent but at odds with other datasets: Here we have data from an evidence source that is internally consistent, but that varies from other evidence sources on this issue.

Compatible with other datasets but internal inconsistencies: The overall thrust of this evidence fits with other sources but lacks some robustness because of certain internal inconsistencies.

Undirected: Isolated data that is neither internally nor externally consistent.

A note on incoming evidence being consistent with what we already know

In examining the evidence, the analyst will also be assessing whether the incoming evidence is *compatible* with prior knowledge on the topic. Does the incoming evidence *fit* with what is already known? By this, we do not necessarily mean that the evidence must agree with existing knowledge. It must just make sense in terms of what we already know.

Thus, sometimes incoming evidence will naturally fit with, and support, existing knowledge. But equally the incoming evidence could *challenge* prior knowledge. But this challenge could still make sense in light of emerging trends and our evolving understanding of the issue.

So, be open minded about how to interpret the compatibility of incoming evidence with what is known already. It could be the incoming evidence is confirming a point. But it also could be telling us something fresh, different and innovative that makes perfect sense and to which we should listen.

Action 3: Identify the Strength of the Evidence

We now look at summarising the analysis of the evidence using the weight, power and direction concepts by establishing the *Strength* of a piece of evidence being used to build your story.

This strength of evidence summary gives us a rounded, informed view of the overall robustness of a piece of data - a key story point - we are using to answer the business question.

The process involves summarising where each piece of evidence critical to our storyline fits in relation to our three concepts - weight, power and direction.

Determining the strength of the evidence is based on a *fuzzy logic* system. This is a mental model for thinking about the data. This is an approach that does not come down to one single statistic that sums up the analysis. It is a framework that allows us to understand complexity even though we do not to have precise mathematically correct measurements for each dimension.

Below we explain how the process of establishing and displaying the strength of evidence.

Summarise the Weight, Power and Direction of the item of evidence in question

Think of the evidence as being distributed across the three weight, power and direction matrices - each of which has four positions: Using this as a mental model for understanding our data we can now work towards establishing the overall strength of the evidence supporting the emerging storyline. To recap:

Weight: tells us about the relationship between *quantitative* support and depth of *qualitative* feeling.

Power: tells us where the evidence stands when assessed against *formal methodological criteria* in relation to our assessment of its *practical track record.* (This reflects our Evaluation and Experience Frames.)

Direction: takes into account the *internal consistency* of the data (such as a series of focus groups) in relation to its *external consistency* (how this data fits with other sources of evidence and our prior knowledge on this topic).

Classify your evidence along the High to Low Strength of Evidence spectrum

Within the Holistic Framework, there are numerous combinations of weight, power and direction scenarios. But do not concern yourself with all the different combinations. Instead we would suggest you use the framework as an overall mental model - a process for guiding your holistic analysis. Start by reflecting on the strength of the evidence in the following way.

Identify High Strength evidence for a story point

This evidence sits in the *top right quadrant* of each of the weight, power and direction matrices. It is characterised by:

High Weight of Evidence: a high proportion are in favour, and they also feel strongly about this topic.

High Power of Evidence: compatible with our classic Evaluation Frame criteria, and also fits with our Experience Frame, which tells us how research evidence works in theory and practice.

Directionally Sound Evidence: the evidence is internally consistent and also externally consistent with other categories of data, together with being compatible with what we already know on this topic.

Identify evidence that is unhelpful in building a story

This evidence essentially sits in the *bottom left quadrant* of each of the weight, power and direction matrices. It is characterised by:

Low Weight of Evidence: low balance of opinion in favour, and also no strong feelings on the topic.

Low Power of Evidence: evidence that is weak in terms of our Evaluation Frame criteria, and also weak when interpreted via our *Experience Frame* lens.

Undirected Evidence: isolated data that is neither internally nor externally consistent.

Identify supporting evidence that could be helpful in building a story point

This is data that sits part way along the spectrum between high strength evidence and evidence that should be rejected because it is not sufficiently robust. Supporting story points will be created using evidence drawn from different places across the three matrices. This is where judgement is required in interpreting evidence that falls into this category.

Set up a Data Wall

One way to summarise what is emerging from our assessment of the strength of different types of evidence - its *overall* weight, power and direction - is to build a *data wall*. The data wall will give you a picture of the pattern of the data.

How people want to work with the data is, of course, a personal decision. Everyone will have their own style of working when it comes to inspecting the different datasets being used to construct a storyline. But we would commend the use of a visual display - the *data wall concept*. Use Post-It Notes as a way of bringing to life the holistic analysis approach.

By beginning to place evidence on a data wall you will have a visual sense of the evidence to which you will be attaching importance in building your story and the evidence that you may decide to downplay.

Building the Data Wall

High strength

Start by identifying all of the available evidence that can be classified as having *high strength*. This will be data that, when passed through our weight, power and direction lenses, is found to be in the *top right-hand corner* of the matrix for each holistic concept. This positioning tells us three important things:

- ¤ The evidence has *Strong Weight* - that is it has strong quantitative support, with lots of depth of feeling being expressed.

- ¤ The evidence has *Strong Power* - that is strong both in terms of our Evaluation Frame and Experience Frame criteria.

- ¤ The evidence is also *Strong Directionally* - it has internal consistency across the different types of evidence and is also consistent with other sources of evidence and prevailing thinking.

In the diagram below we have placed this high strength evidence in the top part of the data wall.

Lower strength

On the bottom part of the data wall we have identified evidence towards the other end of the spectrum - *lower strength*. This is evidence that could come from other combinations of weight, power and direction.

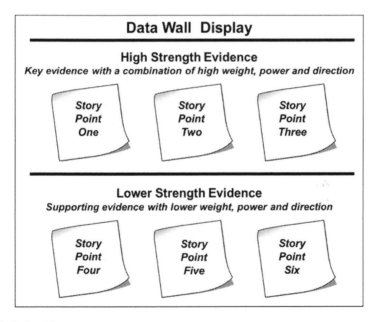

Excluded evidence

It should be noted that we would *exclude* from the data wall the evidence rejected because it is deemed to be low priority, unsafe and undirected (found in the bottom left quadrant of each matrix).

Data Wall example - the changing UK labour market

Let's take the example of building a storyline about the changing structure of the UK labour market and the implications for future employment opportunities.

Identify key story points

The idea is to display the key storyline points in a visual way to help you see the emerging big picture narrative.

The mix of evidence

Here, there are many complex qualitative and quantitative evidence that needs to be assembled to create the story.

What the combination of qualitative and quantitative is telling us

Let's say we had some compelling statistics drawn from a series of *surveys*, each of a robust methodological standard with a large sample sizes, all indicating concerns about the effect of automation on future employment opportunities.

These survey findings are supported by very powerful *qualitative research* evidence highlighting the anxiety that people have about the possibility of losing their jobs. This qualitative research is based on a series of professionally conducted focus groups. It has also been established that there is consistency in the findings across the surveys and focus groups.

The emerging story point

Thus, we have identified a key story point around the growing threat to employment of automation with a set of evidence that has *high weight* (the qual and quant agree), *high power* (the methods are theoretically sound and professionally conducted) and the evidence has *high directional consistency* (it is internally and externally consistent - and in line with prior knowledge).

Record on the Data Wall

This automation's impact on employment story point could now be entered onto the data wall as a piece of high strength evidence.

The next story points

Continue this process by entering onto the data wall the next key story point.

The High Strength story points

All the evidence with high weight, power and direction will be positioned in the high strength part of the data wall display. Having allocated your core blocks of high strength evidence, you can move the Post-It Notes around to get a sense of how the evidence is beginning to address the business question.

The Lower Strength story points

Supporting evidence with lower weight, power and direction can be allocated to the lower strength part of the data wall display. Again, these Post-It Notes can be moved around in crafting the storyline.

Action 4: Identify the most compelling storyline from competing alternatives

The data wall technique will help you get a sense of the strength of the evidence supporting the possible solutions you are considering. This puts you in a good position to start identifying the story options that have the greatest resonance with the overall pattern of the evidence makes most sense in answering the business question.

Below there are some tests to apply in reviewing the different evidence-based storyline options that are emerging.

The common sense storyline test

Ask the following key questions:

- Did you expect this finding?
- Do you believe it intuitively?
- How confident are you explaining this story, given your understanding of the evidence?
- Could you convincingly explain this story to someone who knows nothing about the topic?
- Does this fit with other contextual data that is beginning to support your argument?
- Are there any sources of disbelief around this emerging putative storyline?
- Does the emerging storyline stack up after your application of the seven analysis frames?

The Big Picture storyline test

One way to assess whether you have a compelling story is to test to destruction the strength of the overarching big picture (total sample) storyline. Do not, at this point, worry about variations by subgroup and subplots around the centre of your storyline.

For instance, if this is a study about attitudes of Audi owners towards owning an Audi, concentrate on the main core Audi story. Do not worry about how this story varies by the model of Audi car or by younger/older Audi drivers etc. With most survey data, there is a core storyline that is told through the total sample, with the subgroup variations basically refining this overall storyline. In some cases, there may be two distinctly different storylines at work.

But, as a general rule, there will be an overall storyline. The analyst needs to quickly identify this core story, and test how compelling this is, before getting involved in sub-stories that may be contained within the data.

Test out your storyline:

Roleplay: Roleplay being the stakeholder and ask questions about the data. Make sure you are confident in answering these questions. Can you answer wider *contextual* questions, about the strength of the core evidence underpinning the story? Can you deal with *deep dive* questions about critical points of detail?

The speaking it out loud test: Write your emerging storyline(s) on one page. Then *speak it out* loud to see whether *you* feel comfortable going through the main points. You need to be confident in telling the story to yourself.

Engage with a sounding board: Speak to critical friend to further test how comfortable you are delivering your proposed storyline. Test it to destruction. Specifically, make sure you are convincing when explaining why this central storyline sits above other competing stories you have been reviewing.

Action 5: Build the fluency of your story by using holistic language

Apply holistic concepts to tell your story in a user-friendly and accessible way. Do not just rely on traditional statistical concepts.

However, you may *not* wish to use the actual terms weight, power and direction with stakeholders. These are just terms that we have used to describe a mental model for thinking about complex datasets.

Below we provide some examples the way you could explain each holistic concept to the audience.

Weight of evidence

This could be expressed as:

We consider this evidence to be robust because we found a high proportion of individuals supporting this idea coupled with the positive and passionate way in which many people speak about this.

Power of evidence

This could be explained as:

We are attaching importance to this evidence because it meets all of the research criteria about what constitutes valid, reliable and generalisability of evidence. It is also based on research techniques with a proven track record of practical success.

Direction of evidence

This could be:

We consider this finding to be important because it is directionally consistent across all the different categories of evidence analysed.

A note on the Safety of Evidence concept

A further idea for explaining the holistic analysis approach - building on the concept of the strength of the evidence - is to introduce the idea of evidence being *safe*. The concept of the safety of evidence is used by the legal community as a way of summarising the extent to which it is fair and reasonable to draw a conclusion from a complex mix of hard facts and circumstantial evidence. So, the notion of evidence being *safe* in arriving at a decision could give the insight professional a *language* to explain their craft.

Action 6: Commit to a storyline

The last action of the sensemaking process is to make a final decision on what is the most robust storyline that has emerged from your application of the Seven Frames analysis process. At this point you need to commit to this and start to focus on the best way of telling this story as an evidence-based narrative that will engage the audience.

We pick up this challenge in the next part of the book: *The Insight Story Builder*.

FREQUENTLY ASKED QUESTIONS

Question One: Isn't it risky to be using terms such as *holistic analysis* and/or *sensemaking*, rather than more traditional and familiar methodological terms? Won't this convey the idea that the data analysis process is more impressionistic rather than based on hard-nosed scientific analysis?

Answer: You may or may not want to use the holistic or sensemaking terms to describe the analysis process to your stakeholders. This is a judgement call. However, the notion of talking about the strength of evidence is simple and straightforward to use. Decide whether to use the term safety of the evidence, depending on the audience and the business scenario.

Question Two: Do I have to set up formal weight, power and direction matrices in order to evaluate the evidence or could this be conducted in a more fluid way?

Answer: It could be helpful to formally set up the weight, power and direction matrices, but this is more of a mental model - overall framework - for looking at evidence from different perspectives. Ultimately it is a matter of experimenting with how you wish to apply the framework in practice.

Question Three: Does the holistic analysis framework - using the concept of evidence having weight, power and direction - allow us to include evidence derived from customer transaction and social media sources?

Answer: The holistic analysis framework is helpful in bringing together secondary data sources, qualitative research, quantitative data and also social media listening feedback and customer transaction data. The nature of each of these different evidence sources varies but, looking at each piece of data through the lens of its Weight, Power and Direction remains a helpful way of understanding the evidence.

Top Tip

Be open to the idea of *sensemaking* and thinking *holistically* - quantitatively and qualitatively - about the evidence. Start to experiment - play - with the idea of data having weight, power and direction. Be flexible and pragmatic in the way you use this a *mental model.* Develop a way or working that reflects your own personal style.

Best Next Move

On your next assignment, create a visual data wall to identify the overall Strength of Evidence for each decision option. It will give you an indication of where the strongest evidence lies in order to underpin the key points you are making in creating your solution to the business question.

SUMMARY

The Holistic Frame provides a *mental model* to help you analyse and integrate multiple sources of evidence.

The holistic analysis concepts include the notion of evidence having *Weight, Power* and *Direction*.

¤ **Weight** looks at the relationship between the *quantitative* level, and *qualitative* depth, of support for an idea.

¤ **Power** looks at how our evidence stacks up against classic evaluative criteria and more experienced-based assessment criteria.

¤ **Direction** looks at the consistency within a particular category of evidence together with the consistency of findings across different types of evidence.

We put these concepts together to create the notion of the **Strength of Evidence**, an overall assessment of its robustness. This can be summarised using a visual **data wall** to help identify the most compelling storyline from competing alternatives.

The Holistic Frame opens up the opportunity for a new kind of *language* to make it easier to explain to stakeholders how the sensemaking approach to analysis works.

To conclude this Part of the book we provide a summary of the *Insight Sensemaker Framework*.

The Insight Sensemaker Framework

Decision Frame: How to identify the true business question

Work on the right problem. The creation of a compelling business narrative - and engaging story - hinges on having total clarity around the nature of the business question. Many projects, and subsequent presentations, fail because the analyst only had a hazy outline of the true business question that the project was intended to answer. Often the symptoms of a problem, rather than the true problem, are presented.

Discovery Frame: How to review your data and identify the key evidence

Classify, evaluate and prioritise the available evidence. Quickly get a sense of what evidence is available and how this can be deployed in answering the business question. The skilled analyst will start by building the big picture view of what the overall dataset is telling them. They will review the data to get a sense of the overall findings before ploughing through individual computer tables.

Strategy Frame: How to see the big picture at the start of your analysis

The hallmark of the experienced analyst is to start with the big picture view. But, they then have the flexibility of mind - as they progress through the data - to constantly test to destruction this initial view. This analysis strategy - starting with an initial big picture, then revising this as you make sense of the detailed data - is referred to as the *Hermeneutic Circle* process.

Evaluation Frame: How to establish if your evidence is robust

Assess the robustness of the evidence from the standpoint of classic statistical and methodological principles. Determine how well the evidence you are using to build your story stands up against formal scientific criteria with regard to what constitutes robust evidence. The concepts of validity, reliability and generalisability apply here.

Experience Frame: How to apply your judgement to the analysis

Include your experience of the research process in the evaluation. We need to factor what we know about how customer insight techniques work in practice into our understanding of the evidence. Over the years, research practitioners have built up a body of empirical knowledge that helps us understand what *really* goes on during the research process. It is important to factor this into our interpretation of the evidence.

Enrichment Frame: How to apply creativity to your analysis

Compensate for shortfalls in the data and bring your own experience and creativity to the analysis. Rarely do insights result from the data alone. Insights do not jump off the page and answer the business question by themselves: they emerge from a creative dialogue. The analyst, who is steeped in the evidence and the business question, can add considerable value to the core data by *enhancing* the evidence with their contextual knowledge and point of view.

Holistic Frame: How to build the holistic picture

Make sure you are not presenting building blocks of evidence but have analysed the evidence in a holistic way. Work with the notion of data having Weight, Power and Direction. Put these concepts together to arrive at the overall Strength of the Evidence for your storyline. This allows the analyst to explain the veracity of the evidence in a more accessible way - using terminology such as the Safety of the Evidence.

Summarising your observations

It is helpful to draw together your application of each of the Seven Frames - your main observations and conclusions - into an overall summary framework along the following lines:

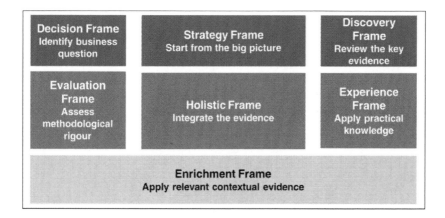

A note on using the Seven Analysis Frames

We recommend that when you first start using the Seven Analysis Frames you work in a sequential way. It is vital to follow the discipline of looking at your evidence through each of the individual frames. However, with experience, you will be able to apply the frames in a more fluid and integrated way.

We move on to Part Two: *The Insight Story Builder*. Based on the evidence you have holistically assembled we will now look at the craft of constructing a compelling narrative.

PART TWO

THE INSIGHT STORY BUILDER

How to construct engaging

customer insight narratives

The Insight Story Builder

We start by demonstrating the power of storytelling in getting over your message and then introduce our *Seven Story Tools*.

The power of narrative in getting over your message

In today's busy and complex communications environment mastering the evidence-based storyteller's craft has never been more important. Being a compelling storyteller who can bring ideas and insights alive is a key skill. People who know exactly how to evoke the emotional power of a story will be the ones able to exert the most influence.

The need for storytelling was particularly evident in the customer insight industry. Over the years, market researchers have often been criticised for providing incoherent, disjointed accounts of isolated chunks of data that did not integrate the evidence and tell a story.

Storytelling was comparatively slow to be accepted as a concept within the world of business. But, over the last few years, storytelling has escalated in popularity. Today, few people need convincing about the power of stories.

Stories are the way we make sense of the world

For example, the ancient Greeks gave us the concepts of ethics, honour, love and retribution, but what we remember is the story of the Trojan Horse. Isaac Newton told us about gravity but what we remember is the story of the apple falling from the tree. The space race was about tense political, scientific and military US and USSR rivalry, but what we remember is the story of Armstrong's first step on the moon.

Some of the reasons why stories are so powerful in helping us get over our message are reviewed below:

Aid comprehension: A coherent narrative means that data is more likely to be understood, absorbed, recalled, and successfully used as part of the decision-making process.

Enrich and involve: Stories are particularly powerful when they are vivid, colourful and use symbols and metaphors that appeal to an audience's emotions and enhance the chances of stakeholders taking action.

Inspirational: Visionary stories can inspire and educate an audience which can help them resolve particular dilemmas.

Communicate the whole picture: Narratives are particularly effective in linking together key relationships in a way that allows individual elements to be remembered as part of a complex whole.

Opportunity to entertain: Stories are especially powerful because they can combine facts with an entertainment factor.

Gain buy-in and encourage sharing: Stories make messages *stick* and are likely to be disseminated - retold and shared - within an organisation.

Enhance actionability: Memorable narratives help to reduce resistance to change and turn insights into action.

A story about the power of stories

History is full of lessons about the importance of being influential and effective in getting over a message. One example is the story of Ignaz Semmelweis.

In 1846 Ignaz Semmelweis began working at the Vienna General Hospital. At the time, there was a very high maternal mortality rate (women dying in childbirth). Semmelweis established that the doctors were contagiously spreading cadaverous particles from performing post mortems prior to treating women in childbirth - without hand cleansing. But no one listened to him.

Semmelweis lacked the communications skills to convince the medical establishment to change their hygiene practice. He was ignored because he was unable to explain what was happening in a compelling and influential way. We had to wait 44 years for Louis Pasteur to tell the story of germ theory.

The Seven Story Tools

Moving away from presenting silos of data towards building a compelling holistic narrative can be rather daunting for many insight professionals. To expect them to become natural storytellers represents a challenge. To address this, we have broken down the storytelling challenge into manageable components.

In the *Insight Story Builder*, we provide Seven Story Tools to help you *tell* the story in a compelling way.

The Seven Story Tools

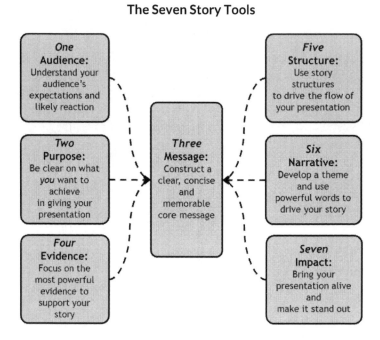

How to work with the Story Tools

We would recommend that you work through *each* of our Seven Story Tools in a *sequential way*. Start by reviewing the Audience Tool, moving on to the Purpose, Message and Evidence Tools. Then continue by working through the Structure, Narrative and Impact Tools.

Once you are familiar with the key principles underpinning each tool, you will find that you are able to apply the tools in a fluid way to build your narrative.

After we have reviewed each of the Seven Story Tools, we demonstrate how to bring them together to create a powerful story using our *Story Builder Framework*.

How we explain each Story Tool

We start by outlining the *Guiding Principles* underpinning each tool. We follow this with the *Key Actions* to apply the tool. Next are some *Frequently Asked Questions*. We follow this with a *Top Tip*. Then there is your *Best Next Move* - ideas on applying the tool to your next project. We conclude with a *Summary*.

We now look at the first of our Story Tools - the *Audience Tool*. This will help to ensure you focus on audience expectations.

8 THE AUDIENCE TOOL
How to understand the expectations and likely reaction of the audience

What follows is a step-by-step guide on ensuring you have a detailed understanding of what the audience is expecting of your presentation. We provide tips on handling different audience scenarios.

GUIDING PRINCIPLES

Principle One: Know what the audience expects from the presentation

Even a well-executed project will fail if insufficient time has been allocated to understanding what it is your audience wants from the presentation. Establish *What's in it for Me* (WIIFM) on behalf of the audience. By knowing your audience, you will be able to answer the critical business question.

Principle Two: Tailor the presentation to the audience's likely receptivity or resistance

Do your homework on your audience so there will not be any surprises that could throw you off on the day of the presentation. Get a sense of whether this audience will be easy to present to, or whether there could be some resistance. Abraham Lincoln said: *'When I get ready to talk to someone I spend two thirds of the time thinking about what they want to hear and one third about what I want to say.*

Principle Three: Make sure your presentation is in the right register

Many presenters often *self-sabotage* their efforts in conducting an excellent project by then failing to allocate enough time to ensure their story will resonate with their audience. Ensure that what you are presenting is in the right *register*. This is one with which the audience will instantly relate and engage. It will not be awkward or at odds with how the audience sees the world. Make sure you use the business language with which they are familiar.

KEY ACTIONS

Action 1: Profile your audience

It is important to obtain as much information as you can about the nature and characteristics of each member of the audience. The counsel of perfection would be to build up the following audience profiles.

Individual profile

Knowing the following may be helpful context - age range, gender mix, nationalities/native languages.

Organisational profile

It can be helpful to find out job titles, seniority, departmental responsibilities, how long they have worked in particular roles and length of service with the organisation.

Project related

What is each audience member's involvement in the project - are they a team leader? Are they tangentially or closely involved?

One way of obtaining information about the audience is to check out stakeholders' *LinkedIn* profiles. This can be supplemented with informal discussions with colleagues about the key players' involvement in the project. But, there could also be a case for questioning stakeholders themselves to establish their personal involvement with the project.

Action 2: Identify the precise expectations of the audience

Explore in detail your audience's exact expectations of your presentation. Put yourself in their shoes and see the presentation through their eyes. How do you think they are likely to think, feel and act in relation to what you are saying?

What overall outcome are they expecting?

Are they expecting you to provide a general contextual piece as background to guide their thinking on an issue? Or, do they want you to frame some of the decision choices open to them? Or, possibly their expectation is that you will make a concrete recommendation between two choices - for example *Do not launch A, go with B.*

A powerful killer question to pinpoint audience's expectations is: On completion of this project, what do you expect to be able to do with the findings - what is the next action you would like to take based on what you will learn from this presentation?

Clarify What's in it for Me (WIIFM)

Building on the *What's in it for Me? (WIIFM)* question that you explored in the Discovery Frame on behalf of the audience, now get total clarity around the concrete, actionable substance they are looking for.

Ask the So What? and Now What? questions

Asking the *So What?* and *Now What?* questions on behalf of the audience will also sharpen your focus. You need establish what the audience will do next once the business question is answered - precisely what do they plan to use your findings for?

Action 3: Establish the audience's involvement with the project

Identify each audience member's emotional involvement with the project. How attached to the outcome are they? Do you know exactly how each audience member will be affected by different outcomes? It is one thing to know an individual's expectations because they are operating in a particular business role, but sometimes you need to go beyond this. Obtain a more deep-seated insight into how their career prospects may be tied up with potential outcomes to the project.

Distinguish *spectators* in the audience - those with low expectations of the presentation because they have little personal *skin in the game* - from those who have invested much emotional energy in the project. If the project fails, their own career could falter.

Some perspectives to explore

- ¤ What kind of project outcome would make an audience member's own position easier and more straightforward?

- ¤ What project outcome or finding would make their own personal position more challenging, difficult or problematic?

You could use the following *projective questioning* techniques to secure insights into what the audience is expecting.

- ¤ What outcomes to this particular project are likely to concern your colleagues?

- ¤ Is it true that some members of the project team believe that certain outcomes to this project will create difficulties for them?

- ¤ What do you think is your colleagues' biggest fear or anxiety about possible outcomes to this project?

By laying off your questions in this projective way, this will enable you to get a richer understanding of audience expectations of your presentation.

Action 4: Identify any hidden or conflicting agendas

There may be hidden agendas that have not been made explicit that you really need to explore so you are not surprised on the day. These hidden issues can sometimes be fairly benign - a stakeholder may simply have forgotten to share a critical piece of information. In other situations, a stakeholder's agenda may be more *Machiavellian* - they may have deliberately not shared information in advance because they have a political agenda.

Thinking global - acting local

Let's take the example of a global organisation that wants to introduce a customer segmentation framework that must be applied in all the local countries in which it operates. The research agency makes the flawed assumption that all the local regions are aligned with this corporate objective. But in fact, several regional locations see the global framework as inhibiting their flexibility.

So, there is really a *global* and a *local* audience for the presentation. By not fully understanding this issue, there is a risk of the presentation failing. In understanding your audience, a general principle to remember is that *however thin you slice it, there are always two sides.*

There are no silver bullet solutions for tackling complex political agendas that could potentially sabotage your presentation. But some specific techniques to try are outlined below.

Paint the Elephant Pink

Often an insight professional may have an idea that there are organisational politics that could undermine the presentation. However, they fail to act on their hunch and instinct. They are then disappointed when these tensions surface during the presentation. If there is likely to be an issue - a potential *elephant in the room* - the advice would be to act. Call it out, highlight it, make it explicit - paint it *pink*! Encourage people to talk about it. By drawing out the issue, you maximise the chances of it being addressed before - not during - your presentation.

The Stakeholder from Hell test

Another useful technique is to do a dry run of your presentation. Ask your colleagues - whom you brief on the potential problems you anticipate - to play the role of the *stakeholder from hell.* Get them to ask lots of problematic questions. By rehearsing in advance how you would handle some of these political complexities, you will be better prepared than just hoping these issues will not surface at all.

Action 5: Touch your audience's world

Touch your audience's world by tapping into the way they like issues presented. There are those whose dominant style is a preference for *visual* stimuli. Others preferred style is listening to detailed verbal (*auditory*) arguments. There will also be those who are more *kinaesthetic* - it is about *how* they feel. There will be audience members who are more *conceptual* - they like big ideas and principles - and those who prefer *practical* concrete examples.

Observe how your stakeholders receive information during the briefing phase of the project (and your various discussions with them). Then mirror and reflect this mix of styles in your presentation.

Speak their language

In addition, get the language right. Many presentations often fail simply because they were in the wrong register and not delivered using the language of the audience.

For example, when presenting to *sales* people, talk about improving sales. If you are addressing financiers, emphasise the extra revenue an initiative could generate. If you are talking to a human resources audience, focus on employee satisfaction.

Action 6: Take personal responsibility for fixing unresolved issues

Do not go into a presentation knowing that there are various issues that have not been completely resolved. Do not hope that these issues will not surface and that everything will be *all right on the night*. Rarely is this the case. Take *personal responsibility* for anticipating and resolving in advance any issues about which you are concerned.

Let's say you have been asked to undertake a study in India and to focus on the major *urban* centres. But throughout you have had worries about whether some audience members may be expecting you to explain the attitudes of those in *rural* areas. Rather than arrive at the presentation with this suddenly becoming an issue, you need to clarify expectations in advance.

It is easy to bury your head in the sand and assume that, because this *problem* is not of your making, it will go away, but this is not usually the case. Because you have not addressed this issue, there could be disappointment on the day of the presentation.

FREQUENTLY ASKED QUESTIONS

Question One: What happens if the audience members are so varied and have completely different expectations, but the stakeholders insist on just *one* presentation output?

> **Answer:** You could make it clear in advance that the presentation has been designed *primarily* for a particular set of stakeholders and explain that there will be further follow-up bespoke presentations for other audiences.

The key is *not* to pretend that these audience challenges do not exist and just hope that everything will turn out all right. You need to take total control of the situation in advance and be prepared to create different presentation decks, for various audiences, in the appropriate format.

Many insight professionals will claim that they do not have the time or resource to do this. But it is a matter of how you prioritise. Highly effective people will find the time and resource in order to guarantee a successful outcome. Less effective people often fudge the issue, with a muddled presentation that satisfies no-one.

Question Two: What strategies and tactics should I follow when there are two audiences for my presentation: those who are attending in person, but also those who cannot attend and will just be reading the presentation afterwards - without the voiceover?

> **Answer:** This is an increasingly common phenomenon. You have designed a presentation that makes sense for the people who will be listening to you. But you also have to think about those who will just be reading the presentation.
>
> Our advice would be to make your top priority ensuring that your verbal presentation will work on the day. Your primary effort should go into making sure your slides work as an accompaniment to what you are saying. You should not be deflected by having to worry about adding extra notes for those who are not there.
>
> The next priority is to deal with the issue of those who cannot attend and will just read the presentation afterwards. Address this by preparing a *separate* document for them - possibly with extra notes. This takes extra time and effort, but it is usually worth it.

Question Three: What strategy and tactics would you recommend in responding to the demands for the presenter to provide a series of deliverables over time, rather than provide a *one-size-fits-all*, once-only presentation at the end of the project?

> **Answer:** This trend towards rolling feedback needs to be embraced. Start by being receptive, not resistant, to the idea of feeding through results on a rolling basis. We are entering a new presentation scenario where there

is less focus on a one-stop, one-size-fits-all, *end-of-project* presentation. Stakeholders now expect to receive a *series* of updates and deliverables over time.

The important point here is that it *is* possible to apply our Story Tools principles to various types of communication - anything from a two-hour presentation right through to a short email. We will return to this later when we have worked through the different Story Tools.

Top Tip

Ensure your presentation provides *actionable substance* that meets the expectations of key stakeholders by doing your homework on the audience. Put in the effort to make sure you can answer the critical *What's in it for Me?* and *So What?* tests on behalf of the audience.

Best Next Move

On your next project, identify the key stakeholders and make sure that you can answer the following questions for each:

- ¤ What do they expect to do with your findings?
- ¤ What do they already know about the subject - what else do they want to know?
- ¤ What opinions do they already have about the subject - and you?
- ¤ Do they have any individual quirks or a hidden agenda?
- ¤ Do they have a preferred presentation style - way of receiving information?
- ¤ How likely is it that they will try to shoot down your arguments?

SUMMARY

The Audience Tool is about putting yourself in the audience's shoes.

Ensure you do *not* walk into a presentation without a comprehensive understanding of the motives and expectations of the audience.

Build a profile of the audience in terms of their organisational role and what makes them *tick*. Identify what is especially important to them.

Touch the audience's world by talking to them in their language.

Unearth any hidden or conflicting agendas that audience members may have.

Do not go into a presentation without fixing unresolved audience issues that could undermine your message.

Our next Story Tool is the *Purpose Tool*. This will help you achieve clarity around exactly what it is that *you* want to achieve in delivering your presentation.

9 THE PURPOSE TOOL
How to be clear on what you want to achieve in giving your presentation

Your *Purpose* is about having total clarity about the change you want to bring about in the audience by giving your presentation. Ensuring that you have a clear sense of purpose about what it is that you, yourself, want to achieve in giving your presentation will encourage you to act with intentionality to achieve a successful outcome.

GUIDING PRINCIPLES

Principle One: Know what change you want to bring about in the audience

You need to make a conscious decision about the difference you want to make by giving this presentation. What change in the audience's behaviour and/or their attitude do you want to bring about?

Principle Two: Your purpose should reflect your stance and what is at stake for you and the stakeholders

In shaping your purpose, be clear on the implications of pursuing your *stance* on the issue, and on what is at *stake* for you and your stakeholders.

Principle Three: Your purpose needs to be clear in your own mind but not necessarily made explicit to the audience

Make sure that *you* are certain about your purpose in giving the presentation. However, you do not necessarily need to make this transparent and explicit to the audience. Everything depends on the scenario.

KEY ACTIONS

Action 1: Be clear on your purpose

Your purpose is about the change you want to bring about in your audience. A lack of purpose is a major reason why presentations - and indeed projects - do not have a successful conclusion. The presenter, at the outset of the project, does not have total clarity around their own purpose - what they themselves want to achieve. Consequently, they do not act with intentionality. Instead they just shuffle into the presentation with only the general aim of concluding the project!

Importantly, purpose is different from answering the business question and/or research objectives.

Your purpose could be to bring about a radical change in thinking amongst stakeholders, so they do not continue to make the mistakes of the past.

Or your purpose could be to make sure stakeholders do not react in a knee-jerk emotional way to the innovative ideas in your presentation.

Or it could be about whether you want stakeholders to shift from having a particular belief or perception to an alternative viewpoint?

It is important to succinctly express your purpose - the change you want to bring about. A good test is to make sure you can crystallise your purpose in a few sentences.

A strategic purpose

There could be scenarios where your purpose will centre on bringing about a radical change in the strategic thinking of the stakeholder audience. For instance, *I wish to change stakeholder thinking from believing that they do not need to shift their position into believing that a major change of direction is now an urgent priority.*

A tactical purpose

You might want to set yourself the purpose of ensuring the audience makes the optimum decision choice. So, your purpose here could be *to ensure that option A is chosen over option B.*

A change in the audience's state of mind

There could be the more complex scenario of changing how people feel about a particular situation. Here your purpose could be *to reduce the fear, anxiety and tension surrounding a particular issue and to leave the audience in a more balanced, informed and less stressed state of mind about making this key decision.*

Action 2: Pinpoint your own personal stance

Insight professionals are expected to influence and add value. It is important that you do not remain neutral. The audience will sense whether you are *authentic, genuine,* and demonstrate *integrity.* Careful prior thinking about your stance is important when presenting your story so that you do not appear hesitant on the day.

Shaping your purpose requires total clarity on your own position - your *stance* on the issue under investigation. A fundamental question to ask here is: *Am I sure about what I believe in and what I am prepared to defend and promote in pursuing my purpose?*

Action 3: Review what is at stake for you

Establish what is personally at *stake* for you - what are the implications and consequences of pursuing your purpose. Is your purpose aligned with your own moral compass? You need to show integrity in balancing the stance you believe you should adopt and the implications of taking this approach.

One consideration is how far you are prepared to take an issue knowing that it could possibly jeopardise your long-term relationship with the client or stakeholder. In some cases, it may be preferable to decline an assignment rather than to compromise what you believe to be your true purpose. On other occasions, more pragmatism is called for. It is all about acting with integrity.

Action 4: Let stakeholder expectations of your presentation inform your purpose

In fashioning your purpose, knowing your stance and what is at stake for you is a start point. But, of course, you also need to reflect your stakeholders' expectations of the presentation. Below we outline some scenarios to illustrate how different contexts can guide your thinking about what you want to achieve - your purpose in giving this presentation.

Updating and contextualising

In this scenario, you could be providing an update to, or a broader contextual understanding of, an existing situation. Here, it is still possible to have a purpose, even though the presentation does not have a specific action outcome. This purpose could be to alert stakeholders not to be complacent in their approach to change.

Generating new thinking

You may have been commissioned to generate fresh thinking and new ideas: the aim is to identify innovative ways of solving a challenge. Here, clearly your purpose would be to provide new ideas that change/improve existing practice - behaviour. However, this could be embellished. For example, if a local business is seeking to go to the next level in providing outstanding customer service, then your purpose could be to encourage the company to be more confident, *think big* and embrace *world-class best practice*.

Go/no go decisions

With this scenario, everything pivots on providing a specific go/no go decision. It is all about giving the green or red light for an initiative. With this type of decision, by having a definite purpose, you will be better placed to advise the audience on the exact action they should be taking to deliver this.

Action 5: Ensure your purpose is sensitive to what is at stake for the audience

Another dimension in shaping your purpose is reflecting on what is at stake for the audience. Building on what you have established in using the Audience Tool, reflect on the effect your presentation will have on stakeholders given their involvement with the project. Below are some client scenarios of which you need to be mindful.

What is at stake for the organisation and its departments?

Identify what a particular outcome is likely to mean for the organisation. If you present recommendation A, does it mean that a business unit would need to close down? Unearth what is at stake and let these insights shape your purpose.

What is at stake professionally for individual careers?

Focus on the implications of different outcomes for the careers of stakeholders - some of whom may have laid their professional reputations on the line in pursuing a course of action. For example, what is at stake for the head of IT in the event of an expensive new installation being abandoned?

Do any outcomes affect stakeholders' personal beliefs?

Reflect on whether your purpose supports or undercuts a deeply held stakeholder belief. For example, how a female company director may feel about the rejection of her initiative for getting more women into senior positions.

Action 6: Decide whether or not you wish to make your purpose explicit to your audience

It is imperative that you have a clear sense of your purpose in your own mind - what change you want to bring about in the audience. But it does not necessarily follow that you want to make this purpose explicit to the stakeholder audience. There are no right or wrongs when it comes to this - it all depends on the scenario.

The avalanche of change facing universities

Let us take the example of a project for a university, where your purpose is to register the vital importance of the university changing its now outdated strategic positioning to a more innovative and radical one. If the university does not change, you genuinely believe it will *not* survive into the future.

Here, the case could be made for being completely explicit and upfront with your purpose at the beginning of the presentation. However, it would also be legitimate *not* to share your purpose with the university in advance. This is because the best way to get buy-in to your message could be to gradually build up your case for the strategic repositioning of the university *before* introducing the idea that *radical* change is required.

FREQUENTLY ASKED QUESTIONS

Question One: Why is having a *purpose* so important to delivering a successful presentation?

> **Answer:** A lack of clarity of purpose is one of the major reasons that insight presentations fail. As the presenter you should go beyond answering the business question and research objectives and be completely clear about what change it is you want to bring about in the audience. This crystallisation of your purpose will become a focal point for achieving a successful project outcome.

Question Two: How can you build the high level of confidence required to always act with intentionality to achieve your purpose? Not everyone has this.

> **Answer:** Being able to crystallise your purpose and relentlessly take action to achieve this - to act with intentionality - does require confidence. But this confidence will flow from working through the seven analysis frames in designing business solutions.

Question Three: Is it possible to achieve your purpose by giving a compelling presentation on the day? Surely having a purpose - changing the behaviour of the audience - also involves considerable consultative follow-up afterwards.

> **Answer:** The construction of a compelling presentation that frames the decision choices will go a long way to achieving the desired change in behaviour. However, the customer insight professional will also need to take various follow-up steps to ensure insights are actioned. We look at this further in the next part of this book *Insights into Action*.

 Top Tip

Clarity of purpose will give you the courage to drive through what you believe needs to be actioned. Think of your purpose as being the North Star that guides everything you do - the golden thread running through the entire analysis and presentation process. Believe in yourself. Do not be hesitant, non-committal and put doubt in the system – express a point of view.

Best Next Move

On your next project, in no more than few sentences, write out your purpose - the change you want to bring about in your audience by giving your presentation. Make sure your purpose reflects your stance on the issue in question and what is at stake for you and the stakeholders. And decide whether you wish to make the purpose explicit to the audience, or whether it is a goal you will work towards in a less overt way.

SUMMARY

The Purpose Tool is about having a clear sense of what change *you* want to bring about in the audience by giving your presentation.

Many projects fail because the insight professional has sleep-walked into the presentation process and never asked themselves: *What do I want to achieve in giving this presentation?*

Clarity of purpose is the hallmark of an effective insight presentation. Having a purpose provides a focus for always acting with *intentionality* to achieve the project's key goals.

Having a purpose is different from solving the business question and/or answering the research aims - it sits above these goals. It reflects the insight professional's stance on the issue and what is at stake for all parties.

The decision on whether or not to make your purpose explicit to stakeholders is a judgement call.

We now look at the *Message Tool*. This will help you to construct a few short sentences that sum up the essence of your presentation.

10 THE MESSAGE TOOL
How to construct a clear, concise and memorable message

Your *Message* is what your audience would say after the presentation if someone (who was not there) asked, *What was that about?* Your message provides a clear statement of how you are addressing the business question.

GUIDING PRINCIPLES

Principle One: Be able to sum up your presentation in a short message

It has been said, *If you can't sum up the story in a sentence, you don't know what you are talking about.* Summing up everything in a concise message increases the chances that your audience will be able to take appropriate action at the end of the presentation. Having a compelling message will also force you to crystallise what it is you want to say. It will also leave the audience in no doubt as to what it is that you represent and stand for. It will make your point of view completely transparent.

Principle Two: Construct a message that makes it easy for your audience to share

A succinct message is more likely to *stick* with your audience. This will also encourage the audience to share the message with others. A concise message becomes a *script* your audience can share with other stakeholders. A clear and memorable message will help you achieve a successful resolution to the business question.

Principle Three: Be clear on when you will make your message explicit to the audience

There is no golden rule about the point at which you will deliver your message during the presentation. It is context and scenario dependent. You need to review the business objectives, the expectations of your audience and the sensitivity of the topic. This will guide you as to the respective merits of *starting* with your message, *ending* with your message or, pursuing other options. One of these other options could be letting the audience *gradually* come to a conclusion about your message for themselves, with you then affirming this with a concise summary of the message.

KEY ACTIONS

Action 1: Craft your message around the business question

The start point for shaping your message is to focus on the business question. Create one concise statement that addresses this core business problem or challenge. Your message should provide the headline - the fundamental conclusion - to your project. It should paint an overall sense of direction but not necessarily outline strategies to deliver this. And it certainly should not get into tactical and operational issues.

Message examples

A government study on the changing structure of the labour market: The dramatic rise in freelance *gig* economy workers and the falling number of corporate sector employees, requires a radical new governmental labour market strategy.

A corporate reputation study conducted for a health food company: We cannot sustain our position as a leading-edge promoter of health and wellbeing if we continue to market brands that have excessively high levels of sugar, salt and fat.

A study conducted on the positioning of a university: An avalanche of change in education is heading our way and, unless the university has a more distinctive strategy to attract more students, it risks bankruptcy.

Action 2: Do not confuse your message with your strategy and/or tactics

Do not become confused between the message you want to deliver and the subsequent strategy and/or tactics you will later explain to stakeholders. It is easy to fall into this trap. Your message needs to give the essence of the business solution, but there is no need to deal with the marketing strategy and tactics for delivering this.

Action 3: Ensure your message reflects your stance and what is at stake for the audience (and you)

It is important that your message is consistent with your stance: it must resonate with what you believe in. Your audience will somehow sense if you are not delivering an authentic message that is grounded in the evidence and in what you believe to be the right thing to do.

When arriving at your final message, also ask yourself whether it is compatible with - and sensitive to - what is at stake for the audience (and you).

Take into account whether your message will be a *bombshell* with massive implications for stakeholders or whether you are delivering good news that will benefit stakeholders.

Action 4: Craft a succinct, clear, memorable message

As a general rule you do not want a message that goes beyond a few sentences. But many insight professionals shy away from distilling down what they want to say into a short message on the grounds that the issue is too complex. This is a mistake. In this era of Twitter - with its 280-character limit - we all need to master the art of crafting a succinct memorable message.

Apply the George Orwell test

Ask yourself whether you could say your message in *fewer words*, with *greater clarity* or in a more *memorable way?*

Concise: Could you cut the number of words in your message. The skill is in knowing what to take out, as much as knowing what to leave in.

Clarity: Could you craft your message in a simpler, easier to understand and intuitive to follow way? Cut any jargon or technical words that are not universally understood.

Memorability: Could you create a powerful communications *hook* that people will remember and share? When Steve Jobs unveiled the iPod, he described his revolutionary new product as *1,000 songs in your pocket.*

Polish your message

Edit down your message to its essence. In the following example - where you have been asked to look at why a company is losing market share and what it should do about it - *Message Take 2* is more memorable than *Message Take 1!*

Message Take 1: Our biggest competitor has reduced our market share - primarily through its claim that it has the lowest prices in town, whilst making some new offers. We could lower our prices to match theirs, but this could be unsuccessful. So, let's discuss whether everyone agrees we should stay as we are with our current strategy.

Message Take 2: Our biggest competitor is grabbing our market share with heavy discounting. Let's keep our nerve: hold our prices but *wow* customers with our quality and service.

Your presentation title is important - think of it as a pledge

Related to the issue of creating a concise and memorable message is your choice of presentation title. Think of this as a kind of *pledge* you are making to your audience.

It is helpful to think of your title as fulfilling your *contract* with your audience to answer their business question. If your title is vague and abstract, then this can suggest that you do not have mastery over what you are going to say.

For example, if your project is about helping a company to be more profitable, and your core findings focus on how increasing staff productivity will deliver this, then your title - pledge - could be: *A guide on how to increase profits by investing in your staff.*

Action 5: Be clear on whether you want to explicitly deliver your message

Decide whether you want to be totally *explicit* with your message or deliver this in a more *implicit* way. Do not leave this to chance. The degree to which you are explicit with your message depends on the circumstances and the nature of the audience. In the majority of situations, the message that you have created is one that you will share with your stakeholder audience at some point.

But on occasion, there could be wisdom in *not* explicitly releasing your message. You could opt for a *softly-softly* strategy, whereby you gradually release elements of the message. You let the audience assimilate the implications of what you are saying. This can offset the feeling that they are being told what to do by an outside consultant.

I am the Greatest!

Angelo Dundee - Muhammad Ali's trainer - often operated without making his message explicit. Ali was an egotist who did not like to be told what to do. So, Dundee would *steer* Ali in a particular direction and allow Ali to gradually come to the conclusion that Dundee's *suggestion* had been Ali's idea all along!

Action 6: Carefully assess at what point you will deliver your message

If you do want to deliver your message at some point in an explicit way, review whether it is best to do this at the beginning, in the middle or at the end of your presentation. There is no simple answer to this. It depends on the audience and the context.

Delivering your message at the beginning

This depends on whether you have a *good news* story (where giving your message at the beginning would work) or a *bad news* story (where having your message at the beginning might get the presentation off on the wrong foot).

A good news story: It can be helpful to release a good news message early. The audience can then sit back and enjoy the way you unfold this core message.

However, one of the dangers of delivering your message at the beginning is that the audience may not let you proceed with the rest of your presentation because they keep asking questions.

A bad news story: Going early with a bad news message may ruffle feathers and panic people. The audience may start to derail the presentation by challenging you in an aggressive way about what they may perceive to be a threatening message. They may not let you get to some of the nuances and important complexities that it would be sensible to explain before releasing your final recommendation.

Delivering your message midway

Some audiences could favour listening to some background context, then being introduced to your message. This approach allows them time to then reflect on the message during the remainder of the presentation.

Releasing your message at the end

This works when you need to:

Gain buy-in: Provide to the evidence that corroborates your story *before* providing what could be a surprising or unexpected conclusion or recommendation.

Pave the way for delivering a bad news story: Here, if you hit the audience with bad news too early, they could react by challenging your credibility. They could attack the messenger, not the message.

Ensure the audience will not switch off to the rest of your presentation once you have previewed the overall findings via your message.

FREQUENTLY ASKED QUESTIONS

Question One: Why is having a *message* so critically important in business communications?

>**Answer:** A succinct, memorable message will offset the likelihood of hasty or sub-optimum *processing* of your presentation. Some stakeholders will just absorb your information for later decision-making. Others may be making *real-time* decisions based on your presentation findings. And,

others may use a mix of these approaches. A crystal clear message will minimise the chances of the audience getting the wrong idea of what you are trying to communicate.

Question Two: Is there any real difference between your *purpose* and your *message*?

> **Answer:** These are totally different concepts. The message sums up what you say in the presentation to answer to the business question. Your message is what you would say to someone who was not at the presentation if they asked you to briefly say what the presentation was all about.
>
> Your purpose is about what change in behaviour you want to bring about in the audience as a result of them understanding this fundamental message.
>
> For example, for a university audience, your *message* might be that their university is facing a threat to its long-term survival. But your *purpose* is different. This could be to galvanise the university into taking immediate radical action to address the various disrupters to their current business model.

Question Three: Are there ever situations where the same presentation can have more than one message?

> **Answer:** A presentation can more than one message. Let's take the example of a project to help an ailing newspaper secure its future. Here there could be a key *strategic-level* message, designed primarily for the Board of Directors. This addresses the strategy for delivering the newspaper online over time, whilst also providing a print copy version. But, there could also be a message for the *editorial team* about improving the content for the target audience. And there may even be a third message aimed at the *marketing team* about improving the newspaper's promotional and pricing strategies.
>
> In situations where there are different messages for various audiences, review carefully whether you can do this in one presentation or whether you need to have separate presentations. For example, with the newspaper illustration, a case could be made for delivering your three

messages to a composite audience. But there could also be a case for a headline presentation, with separate follow-up presentations to the Board of Directors, editorial team and marketing team.

Top Tip

Sharpen and polish your message by testing it out with a critical friend who knows nothing about the background to the project. Based on this feedback, keep refining your message until it becomes the most impactful way of registering your point.

Best Next Move

On your next project, make sure your message sums up your presentation in a few short sentences. Does it pass the George Orwell test? Could you make this more concise (say it with greater economy - fewer words)? Could you add more clarity (get over your point in an easier or more straightforward way)? And, could you make this message more memorable? This technique will help your message stick and encourage people to share it with others.

SUMMARY

The Message Tool focuses on what your audience would say to someone who was not there, if asked *What was the presentation about?*

In today's busy communications environment, being able to sum up your presentation in a short statement is critical. Having a message lies at the heart of effective storytelling.

It is important that your message squares with what you believe the evidence is telling you - your stance - and what is at stake for the audience and you.

Polish your message so that it is clear, concise and memorable. Decide where in the presentation - the beginning, middle or end - you will make your message explicit.

Next, we have the *Evidence Story Tool*. This focuses on identifying the killer evidence you will select to underpin your storyline.

11 THE EVIDENCE TOOL
How to focus on the most powerful evidence to support your story

The aim of the *Evidence Tool* is to identify the most powerful, compelling and persuasive killer evidence that will drive your storyline.

Great storytellers get over their message with a minimum of evidence. They know how to provide the evidence that will ensure their argument *stands up*. But they do this without running the risk of data overload.

Be ruthless in deciding what evidence supports your narrative and will most likely to influence the audience. Focus on the evidence that will build the credibility of your narrative.

GUIDING PRINCIPLES

Principle One: Apply the Less is More rule - focus on the key evidence

It is usually possible to communicate the lion's share of your story using only 20% of the data. Do not subscribe to the idea that, to answer the business question, you must present *all* the data you have collected.

Principle Two: Select evidence that best supports your message

Focus on the evidence that is most relevant to answering the business question and most likely to capture the imagination of the audience. It is helpful to apply the principle of the *Commander's Intent*. Great Commanders know that, in the heat of war, detailed battle plans become blurred. So, they ensure that there is one main objective that every soldier can remember.

Following this principle, focus on the key pieces of evidence that you most want the audience to take away from your presentation.

Principle Three: Win the rational **and** emotional argument

Select the evidence that taps into the way your audience *thinks,* and how they *feel,* about the topic. This approach will also encourage the audience to *act* on what you are saying.

KEY ACTIONS

Action 1: Select the killer evidence most relevant to the business question

In choosing your key evidence, focus on the evidence that is most relevant and compelling in answering the business question. What is it that your audience most needs to know to answer this business issue?

Focus on the Main Thing

Select evidence that elegantly and succinctly addresses the core business question - the *main thing.* Do not be deflected into providing endless amounts of data that address different supporting research objectives. Provide a *golden thread* of relevant and impactful evidence that runs through your storyline. Work relentlessly towards answering the business question. This discipline will give your presentation a *spine* and avoid it being seen as disjointed.

Answer the business question

For example, if the business question is whether the organisation should expand into China or not, then provide data that answers this business question. This is the *main thing.* Do not for instance provide an excess of contextual information about relative economic prosperity of different neighbouring Asian countries.

Go for the killer stat

For example, if your point is about gender inequality - women struggling to break the *glass ceiling* - then look for an eye-catching *killer* stat to drive home your point. This could be along the lines of, *Amongst the world's top companies, only around 6% have women CEOs.*

Action 2: Keep it Simple - distinguish complexity from confusion

Natural storytellers keep it simple. Know when to respond to a *complexity*, and when to avoid getting drawn into *confusing* side issues. Good storytellers know the difference between a genuine complexity - that must be resolved to sustain credibility - and an irrelevant confusion that should be eliminated.

By complexity, we are talking about an issue that must to be addressed to arrive at an informed, rather than naive, solution to a business question. This is different from a confusing side issue that deflects attention from answering the business question.

Must know - not nice to know

For example, in a presentation to a start-up business about how to set up an online marketing system, an important complexity is explaining the fundamental rules about spam emailing. Get this wrong and the company could receive big fines from the data protection regulators. So, these rules must be addressed. But you do not have to go into the detailed legal technicalities - this would just confuse.

Action 3: Focus on the Wow evidence

Identify the *wow* evidence that will bring your point alive. Focus on the evidence that is most likely to *stick*, be remembered and shared with others. Select the evidence that taps into the way the audience thinks and feels.

To drive your story home, provide powerful and memorable communications *hooks* to reinforce your key evidence. This will make it easier for people to remember - and share your story with others. For example, many still remember *9 out of 10 cats prefer Whiskas!*

Learn from great journalists

A good yardstick to judge whether you have cut through to create a compelling evidence-based storyline is to compare yourself with top journalists. They advance a complex argument with just the right amount of evidence: no more - no less. You can always tell a good journalist because they always provide *just enough* facts to convince their readers about the robustness of their piece. The narrative is elegantly written with the appropriate level of information needed to build credibility and authority.

In contrast, poor journalism has difficult to access, densely written text coupled with insufficient substantiating facts. This leads the reader to immediately question - and reject - the central argument.

Action 4: Touch the audience's world - use familiar business heuristics

Select the evidence that will touch your audience's world. This should provide a blend of evidence to engage at an intellectual and emotional level.

Tap into familiar business heuristics - rules of thumb - that stakeholders use to make sense of the world. Thus, with a finance audience, focusing on frameworks and metrics around the revenue and profit that a new product might generate will pay dividends. For a marketing audience focus on website traffic, social media likes, and landing page engagement.

Action 5: Present simple intuitive and visual solutions

Some audience members respond better to visual, others to audio, and some to more kinaesthetic cues. The aim should be to take a complex *data-centric problem* and convert this into an *intuitive visual solution*.

Below is data that shows how candidates for a job performed on two tests:

Test One - Team player: Whether they are a good team player or not.
Test Two - Problem solving: Whether they are good at problem solving or not.

From a data-centric cognitive problem to an intuitive visual solution

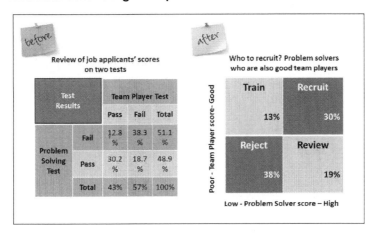

The table to the left sets up a data-centric cognitive problem. But it is difficult to work out the story from these numbers. In contrast, the graphic to the right is an intuitive visual solution. This immediately tells the story: who you should recruit, who you should reject, who you should train and who you should review.

Action 6: Be prepared with supporting evidence

There could be certain critical complexities that a stakeholder may raise at the presentation that you need to address by providing supporting evidence.

Therefore, ensure you have easy access to this key supporting evidence - via an annex or hyperlink. However, ensure your story flows and is not disrupted by too much switching between the main story and data in an annex.

In deciding what evidence might be needed to support your main point, set up a role play with a *critical friend* to establish what it is reasonable for a stakeholder to ask about your storyline. Use this feedback to decide what annexes and/or hyperlinks might be required, and to rehearse your answers to likely questions.

FREQUENTLY ASKED QUESTIONS

Question One: Why do so many insight professionals fail to tell their story with just the minimum of data?

> **Answer:** Insight professionals often believe that they will be judged on the amount of effort they put into assembling huge amounts of research data. But in reality, they will be judged on the power and simplicity of their final output - their story. The start-point for addressing this (over) anxiety to please by showing every piece of data is to recognise that often *less is more*. You need to keep it simple. So, it comes down to showing some courage!

Question Two: What if the audience's expectations and demands are so varied and fragmented that it is impossible to be selective in the evidence used?

> **Answer:** It can be tempting to throw in the *kitchen sink* and bombard the audience with absolutely everything. But this shows intellectual laziness.

The first issue is to decide whether or not giving only *one* presentation is the best way forward. If so, then commit to making this work. If not, summon up the energy to prepare bespoke presentations to meet different audience expectations.

Question Three: How do I make sure I don't *oversimplify* complex issues?

Answer: It comes down to judgement. It is sometimes said that, *Brevity may be the soul of wit, but it can be the death of meaning*. So, it is about finding the *sweet spot*. One approach is to experiment - play with - ways of reducing the data mass without undercutting the strength (and also subtlety) of the issue you are addressing. Dramatists and novelists - storytellers - will spend hours editing down their material. They will experiment with what *works* before eventually arriving at the most powerful and simple way of making their point.

 Top Tip

You are not being paid by the hour for work done, but for providing a *transformational solution to the business problem*. Have the courage and belief in the value of refining the evidence down to its absolute core essence. You will not be judged by how much effort you put into preparing the presentation but by your solution. Apply *forensic energy* - constantly ask yourself how you can ruthlessly edit down, refine and polish the initial data outputs. Commit to transforming these into an impactful, concise and memorable story.

 Best Next Move

On your next project, identify the most powerful data that best tells your story. Force yourself out of the habit of simply plucking data for your presentation from computer tables in the form that they were originally generated. Be ruthless in editing down and integrating the evidence. Make sure you are presenting a *mix* of evidence to engage with how the audience thinks, and also feels, about the issue. You need to win the *hearts and minds* of the audience.

SUMMARY

The Evidence Tool is about reducing the data down to its core essence.

Create a compelling easy-to-follow narrative, underpinned with just the right amount of supporting evidence to convince stakeholders of the veracity of your argument.

Select with integrity the key evidence that most faithfully and elegantly tells the story.

Keep the evidence simple and be able to distinguish *complexity* from *confusion*.

Touch the audience's world by winning the rational *and* emotional argument. Use business heuristics and frameworks with which the audience is familiar..

Focus on *wow* evidence that will stick in the audience's mind and provide communications hooks around which to build your storyline.

Present simple intuitive visual solutions, not data-centric problems.

Put supporting evidence in an annex.

Next, we look at the *Structure Tool*. We provide a number of structures you could consider in building your storyline.

12 THE STRUCTURE TOOL
How to use Story Structures to drive the flow of your presentation

Structure lies at the heart of creating a compelling story. An elegant story structure will ensure you are communicating with your audience in *storytelling* mode, not just dumping data.

A coherent structure sets the context, drives the flow of your presentation and organises ideas into categories to make it easier for the audience to understand your message. When a sound structure is in place, you do not notice it: you take it for granted. But, when there is a lack of structure, this creates a disconnect which can irritate the audience.

GUIDING PRINCIPLES

Principle One: There is an architecture to an elegant story

Think of your presentation as having an overall architecture that drives the *flow* of your story. It will be a narrative that *arcs* from your introduction through to a conclusion. Your structure should take the audience on a journey (as in a film or play). And at different points in your story, create *lean-in* moments where you strike a powerful emotional chord.

I Have a Dream

An example of the power of structure can be found in Martin Luther King's *I Have a Dream* speech. This speech has a distinct *architecture*. First, he sets up a *challenge (problem)* - that is the black community in the US are being treated unfairly. Then he moves on to discuss *a solution* - the arrival of the Civil Rights movement campaigning for equality. He then has a *call to action,* which he brilliantly articulates through his compelling *I have a dream* message.

Principle Two: Do not default to creating a data building block presentation

Do not fall into the habit of creating a presentation that is no more than blocks of evidence drawn from different phases of the research process. Instead, create an attacking narrative that integrates all the evidence into a compelling story.

The building block approach is the way many of us begin to assemble our evidence. But your final structure must go beyond simply presenting isolated strands of evidence with just a tenuous link to some form of conclusion. You need a structure that integrates the evidence, creating a flowing story that holds the audience's attention.

Below, we show what a pedestrian *building block* structure looks like, and then compare this to an *attacking narrative* where the evidence is integrated into a storyline that answers the business question.

The data building block approach

This approach does *not* have any of the ingredients of compelling storytelling. It simply plods through a set of data one block after another. It does not connect together different pieces of evidence - join up the dots.

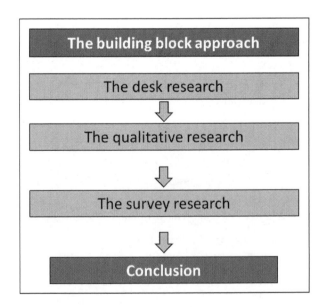

The attacking narrative approach

An attacking structure is one where the evidence does not sit in isolated data silos but has been drawn together and feeds into a storyline. This will keep the audience engaged as you work through the way to resolve the challenge, tension or dilemma underpinning the business question.

This approach is the hallmark of great storytelling. It integrates the evidence and sustains the audience's interest and engagement. It takes them on a journey that leads them towards the decisions they need to take.

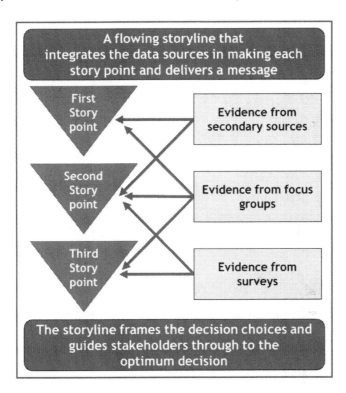

Principle Three: Experiment with different structures (and substructures) to arrive at the optimum story flow

Often there is no one right structure. But your presentation must have one. Experiment with the most compelling structure to answer the business question. Play with various ways of telling your story using different structures (and substructures). This experimentation will help you arrive at the most impactful structure for delivering your message.

KEY ACTIONS

We review story structures that you may wish to use to deliver your message. They are food for thought. They are not the only storytelling structures available but provide a selection of ideas with which to experiment.

The story structures we cover will help ensure you meet three key criteria of sound storytelling. First, focus on the conflict, tension, or issue - the business question - that the audience expects to be addressed. Second, integrate the key evidence: connect everything and do not present random disjointed points. And third, take the audience on a journey towards a resolution, where the consequences of taking different actions will be clearly framed.

Specifically, it is helpful to work through the following six actions - each of which focuses on a particular story structure. For each we provide a summary, and then offer guidance on when to use this approach - how to play to its strengths and limitations.

Action 1: Review the Linear Structure options

Linear Story Structures take the audience on a journey leading to a resolution. This type of structure works well because it is familiar. People have an innate interest in wanting to find out what happens next. Below we outline some variations of the linear structure.

Linear Structure One: Background/Confrontation/Resolution

This structure starts by outlining the critical *Background* needed to understand the story you are about to tell. It then deals with the central conflict or *Confrontation* at the heart of the business question. It then moves to ways of *Resolving* this issue.

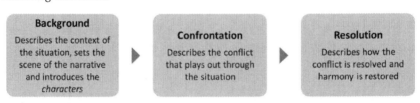

This structure lends itself to scenarios where existing business practices that have been working well are challenged. It works when it is important to explain critical context, history or background <u>before</u> outlining the subsequent confrontation and resolution.

Illustration: A long-standing retail business model comes under threat

A retailer with a successful track record of trading in the value-for-money space is now confronted by a competitor that starts beating them on price *and* quality. This leads to a strategic appraisal of their business model. Here, mapping out the *Background* - to draw out what has worked well in the past - is an important part of how you will tell the story. You do this *before* addressing the *Confrontation* of the competitive disruptor - and then you go on to the *Resolution*.

Linear Structure Two: Challenge/Solution/Call-to-Action

This structure starts by focusing on a specific *Challenge* - rather than first talking about the background to the problem. Then you present the *Solution* that then leads to a *Call to Action*. This approach was Steve Jobs' simple but effective go-to structure. Typically, he would present a challenge/problem, then provide the solution, and then set up a call to action.

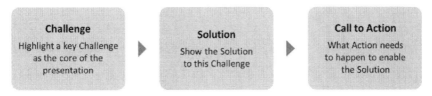

This structure works well when there is a widely acknowledged challenge that can be addressed without the prior need for the background to be mapped out. This structure immediately engages the audience with the importance of the challenge, then proceeds to the solution and the call-to-action.

Illustration: A sudden change in the rules becomes a game changer

Due to unexpected political tensions, the government decrees that a company can no longer trade with a specific country (the *Challenge*). The company needs to replace this lost revenue by trading with other countries (the *Solution*). This leads to the *Call to Action*, which could be the introduction of a major global advertising campaign.

Linear Structure Three: Situation/Complexity/Resolution (Q&A)

The *Situation/Complexity/Resolution* structure sets out the business *Situation*, and then deals with important *Complexities*, before outlining the *Resolution*. The *Resolution* is often addressed in the form of *questions* that are then *answered*.

This structure begins with a critical analysis of the business situation. You then introduce key complexities that *must* be addressed before a *resolution* can be found. It is essential that you do *not* get drawn into explaining unnecessary confusion. Only highlight the complexities that must be solved to deal with this business question. The complexities could cover business considerations, methodological issues, or project execution factors. Then there is your resolution - possibly presented as answers to the business question.

It is vital that you are completely clear on the difference between a genuine *complexity* that must be addressed and a *confusion* that will distract you from you telling your story.

This structure lends itself well where there is an inherent complexity. But it is not appropriate where there is little or no complexity to unravel and explain to the audience.

Illustration: The local team are not on-side

A major global brand is rolling out to local regions a new worldwide marketing communications strategy with a radically different brand message. But in many local regions there is strong resistance to this idea. They believe that the new global brand message has too much of an impersonal global feel and does not respect local sensitivities.

This is critical *Complexity* that must be addressed in telling the story. The *Situation/Complexity/Resolution* structure allows this critical complexity - the global vs local tension - to be factored into the presentation.

Action 2: Review the Nonlinear Structure options

A nonlinear structure refers focuses on a core concept, idea or key statistic and then builds the story outwards from this *big idea*. This structure only works when there is a powerful core concept at the heart of the findings. You structure your entire storyline around this central construct, addressing different perspectives that flow from this core idea.

This concept or core idea could be, for example, the notion of improving customer loyalty, or boosting productivity, or enhancing profitability. It is this core concept that sits at the heart of the presentation. You then look at this from different perspectives. Below we outline some different non-linear structures.

Nonlinear Structure One: High-Level Concept

The *High-Level Concept* structure has a central concept sitting at the heart of the presentation with there being different perspectives that you then address. These could cover looking at the *context* to this issue, looking at *variations* around the core idea, doing a *deep dive* to explore specific aspects of this idea, or looking at the issue from *different viewpoints*.

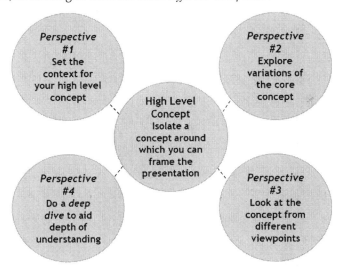

In using this approach, ensure there is a sufficiently powerful *core concept* the audience will be interested in you exploring. This structure often appeals to senior audiences who like to cut through to the heart of answering a problem by focusing on fundamental concepts and core drivers of success.

Illustration: Exploring the concept of entrepreneurial behaviour

Let's say you are exploring how to build a more entrepreneurial economy. Here the core concept could be *The Entrepreneurial Mindset*. The presentation puts at its heart the characteristics of successful entrepreneurial behaviour - and then looks at this from different perspectives.

It is important to point out that - with the nonlinear *High-Level Concept* structure - within any one *subset* of the content, each point will be advanced in a sequential (*linear*) way.

Nonlinear Structure Two: Lead/Support/Tail

The *Lead/Support/Tail* Structure pivots around there being a killer statistic (or central argument) that essentially tells the story. This structure is nonlinear because it centres around a few key statistics. It zeros in on a *killer* statistic which is followed by a key piece of supporting data and selected additional data. These statistics drive the entire story.

- Start at the highest level of generality with a *core assertion* statement showing the *Lead,* headline killer evidence about the fundamental point you are making.
- At the next level, you move to *Supporting data* to further validate and/or add texture and richness to your core assertion.
- Finally, there will be additional data to further embellish your argument - the *Tail*.

This structure is often used by newspaper journalists.

- At the top of the story they *Lead* with an eye-catching *headline* statistic.
- They then funnel down to provide one key *Supporting* fact.
- They will end in the *Tail* by providing one or two related, but less critical, facts.

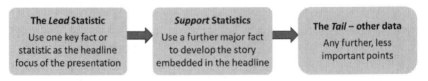

The *Lead* Statistic — Use one key fact or statistic as the headline focus of the presentation → *Support* Statistics — Use a further major fact to develop the story embedded in the headline → The *Tail* – other data — Any further, less important points

This structure works well when you can deliver your message around a small number of key statistics. It requires a genuine stand-out statistic about how customers think and/or act. It cannot just be a mildly interesting observation.

Illustration: Is obesity killing the next generation?

An example of this approach would be: 75% of children from a certain region were obese (the *Lead* headline statistic). This would be followed by supporting statistics, such as only 10% of children now do any form of regular exercise *(Supporting statistic)*. There would then be further statistics, such as 40% of kids spend over three hours a day playing video games and/or being on social media (the *Tail*).

Thus, this nonlinear structure is in contrast to linear structures where you would start with a beginning (background, challenge or situation), progress to a middle (confrontation, solution or complexity) and then to an end (with resolution, call -to-action or questions answered).

Nonlinear Structure Three: Interactive

Another nonlinear structure is the *Interactive* storytelling technique. This involves starting by presenting your fundamental message. You will have all the material pre-prepared, but the audience decide the order in which they want you to examine various perspectives to this message.

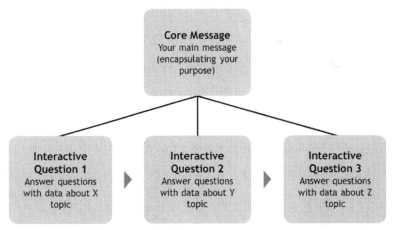

This is an approach that allows a senior audience to quickly grasp the core message and then - via questioning - to *pick & mix* their way through the issues upon which they want to focus. It is a technique for the experienced presenter comfortable dealing with a senior audience that favours this interactive style.

Illustration: A university student satisfaction study

Your core message is that a university is bottom of the league table in terms of student ratings of its standard of teaching. It needs to radically improve its performance if it is to survive. You explain to the audience that you have analysed the teaching satisfaction scores by different categories of student, and other factors, and are prepared to take questions. Thus, your structure is driven by what are the priority issues for the audience. The process could be:

- A first set of questions about how satisfaction ratings vary by faculty: is it worse for arts or the sciences and so on?
- The next questions could be about whether student scores on teaching standards vary by the different campuses/sites at which the university is based.
- There could then be questions around whether the student scores vary depending on the number of students in the class.

Action 3: Review the Substructure options

To support your core structure, it can be helpful to introduce various *substructures* to highlight specific elements of your storyline. These substructures can be incorporated into your overarching structure - either linear or nonlinear.

Play around with how you might use certain substructures *within* your overall structure on your next presentation.

Below, we briefly summarise some story substructures and provide advice on when it is best to use each substructure.

The Time Machine

This substructure paints a picture of what the future would look like if the audience decided to follow a particular course of action. It provides a kind of *springboard into the future* and illustrates with clarity the likely outcome of the decision.

Illustration: What would our corporate reputation look like in five years' time if we sponsor the X Premiership football club

For example, what is the likely future impact if an organisation decides to become the main club sponsor of a Premiership football club? What will happen if it has its logo on the players' shirts and renames the stadium after the company? We could show what the corporate reputation of the sponsoring organisation might look like at the end of a 5-year sponsorship deal.

The Parallel Universe

The Parallel Universe substructure allows you to review - in parallel - the implications of going forward with alternative or competing business scenarios.

Illustration: Investing in the UK or the US?

Let's say the issue is whether to expand the UK operation or use this money to open a new business in the USA. One part of the storyline would be around *what could happen if we invest in the UK*. You would accompany this with *what the future could look like in terms of a new US venture*.

The Comparison

This simple technique can sharpen the analysis of an issue by reviewing where there are *similarities,* and where there are *differences*. Many audiences will be familiar with this *Compare & Contrast* analysis technique.

Illustration: What do we do better, the same or worse?

You could use this technique as a way of evaluating your own company against a competitor. Specifically, you would identify what the competitor *does better than you (and differently)* and what it is that both you and the competitor do that is *virtually the same*. And then pinpoint what it is that your *own company does better than the competitor*.

By looking at the issue from this perspective you are often able to highlight opportunities to gain a competitive advantage.

The Counterpoint Story

This substructure is useful where there is *received* - but necessarily substantiated - *wisdom* circulating around a topic. Use this to jolt the audience out of slavishly accepting this point of view. This approach involves risk and needs to be used sparingly, but it can be engaging. You need to think carefully before considering this as a possible substructure to support your overall storyline.

Illustration: We are no longer the best!

Let's say a city is claiming to be the *world's most popular holiday destination* - but is this really true? With this substructure you begin to unfold some home truths. Other holiday destinations are now better able to make the claim that *they* are the world's favourite holiday spot. You then introduce ideas on how to reclaim the top holiday destination accolade.

The Reverse Story

The Reverse Story is about starting at the *end* of an event and working back to the beginning. In certain communications scenarios this could be a way of engaging the audience.

Occasionally dramatists use this idea - Harold Pinter's play *Betrayal* is an example. The play starts at the end, with the two central characters discussing the *end* of their relationship and works back to the beginning to how they first met. This substructure should be used only when it is entirely appropriate.

Illustration: How can we learn from the mistakes of the past?

The *Reverse Story* approach could work for a business that has got into difficulties. You could focus on the current situation. Then work back to trace the critical points where action should have been taken to avoid running into trouble. This provides a lens through which to highlight lessons for the future. It puts the spotlight on key watch-outs to avoid these mistakes happening again.

For instance, let's say a major grocery chain had to close some of its flagship supermarkets. You could start the presentation with the latest store closure and work backwards to its opening day, explaining what went wrong during the life of this store. Then you could develop a theme around *making sure history doesn't repeat itself.*

Action 4: Using signposting techniques to signal your story flow

Support your structure (and substructures) with signposting techniques. The audience's concentration can wander - they start checking their emails! But signposting will help regain their attention by providing a clear *roadmap* of the presentation *journey*. You give the audience *cues* as to where you are in the presentation.

Below are some techniques to help you organise your presentation narrative.

Signpost your overall structure

An engaging presentation title that reinforces your message (and sets out your *pledge*).

The Contents page is a key scene-setting technique - it starts to tell the story.

Simple numbering devices for example, Part One - Step 2 - Issue iii.

Signal where you are in your running order

A flysheet to indicate the start of a new part of the story.

A summary panel showing your presentation subsections indicating - on a rolling basis - what has been covered to signal where you are in the presentation

Introduce recap pages: Tell them what you are going to say, say it, and then tell them that you have said it.

Highlight elements of the presentation content

Colour coding to highlight parts of your story. For example, a specific colour will refer to a particular topic.

Icons to instantly identify a concept. For example, a *Gold Star* icon could represent a premium customer.

Maps and diagrammatic devices help - for example a UK map highlighting the region you are discussing.

Action 5: Use Storyboarding to arrive at the optimum structure

The storyboarding technique - using Post-It Notes - can be extremely effective. This allows you to experiment with different structures, substructures and ordering techniques to see how they might work together in the most fluent way.

Using the storyboarding technique

Think it: Write on a Post-It Note a sentence to describe each point you wish to make.

See it: Pin up the Post-It Notes in the order you wrote them. Then talk yourself through each one and see how the story flows.

Do it: Play around with your initial running order until you feel comfortable with the flow. Talk through the emerging storyline until you feel confident in your narrative.

Pick a horse and ride it!

One final tip - we recommend playing around with different structures. But there is rarely just one right structure. So, you must eventually settle on one - then stick to it. You will reach a point where there will be diminishing returns with further experimentation. You need to *pick a horse and ride it*: select a structure, stay with this and make this structure work.

Storyboarding will help to ensure the story flows

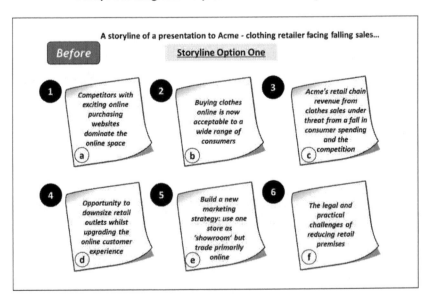

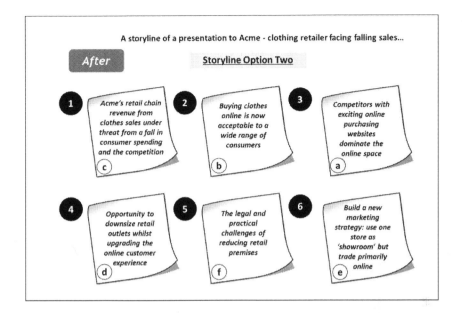

Action 6: Apply Story Tools thinking to all insight communications

Today there are various options in the communications deliverables toolbag including:

- Face-to-face 30-minute verbal presentation
- High-level one-to-one executive summary of key findings - by phone
- A tele-conference remote presentation for a team of people
- A pre-read presentation - to be studied ahead of a verbal presentation
- A standalone presentation/report to be read without any presenter input
- An implementation workshop to take place after a pre-read presentation
- A follow-up diagnostic workshop to deal with any complexities arising from the earlier rolling feedback

Given this, it is important to recognise that our storytelling principles apply to everything from a major face-to-face presentation through to emails. So, it is important to know how to apply the Story Tools to different types of communication.

How to tell the story in an email!

One important test of your storytelling skills is whether you can apply the Story Tools in an *email!*

To: The CEO
From: Head of Insight
Subject: Good news from recent concept test
Attached: Concept test data

Hi CEO
The data from the concept test is attached - the key message is that this is good news.
As you predicted, execution X performed best - well ahead of your action standard.
We strongly agree with you about moving ahead with X.
Here is one of the verbatims about execution X 'Wow. . . A non-alcoholic whisky flavoured beer for adults! What a great idea. . . Looking forward to trying this when it comes out'.
As you can see, people picked up all the key messages and were enthused.
The execution did well with women 18-25 - they look like being the target market.
I will call you to discuss the findings and recommendations further.

Regards
CJ

FREQUENTLY ASKED QUESTIONS

Question One: What is the best process to follow in choosing the optimum structure for my presentation structure?

    Answer: There are the following elements to this:

- ¤ The start point is to carefully review the Audience, Purpose, Message and Evidence Tools so you are clear about your audience's expectations, what you want to achieve (your purpose), your key message, and the nature of the killer evidence.

¤ Next, *review the different linear and nonlinear story Structures:* explore which structure best delivers your message and will *stick* with the audience.

¤ Then explore opportunities to use certain *substructures.*

¤ Use the storyboarding technique to visually experiment with different storylines.

¤ Then rehearse your preferred storyline structure (with substructures) by reading it out loud and listen to how it sounds and feels as you deliver it.

¤ When you reach a point where you feel the story narrative *works,* stop and settle on a structure. At this point do *not* keep revisiting your chosen structure.

¤ It now becomes a matter of *picking a horse,* then knowing how to *ride it.*

Question Two: Is it the case that there is always one structure that is incontestably better than any other structure?

Answer: Often there could be several structures that would work equally well. Thus, a presentation using the *Situation/Complexity/Resolution* structure could work equally as well as the *Background/ Challenge/Solution* structure. But, avoid having a structure that demonstrably does *not* fit the problem - a structure that makes your delivery of the presentation an uphill battle.

Question Three: How do I decide what substructures to integrate with the main story structure?

Answer: There is no golden rule. But substructures are helpful at a critical point in your story where it is vital to drive home the implications of an insight. Experiment with different substructures to determine which ones are going to serve you best in building your story.

 Top Tip

Use storyboarding - *Visual Displayed Thinking* - to help you experiment with what story structure will work best. Set up a storyboard - using Post-It Notes - and play around with different options until you arrive at the one you feel flows most naturally.

Best Next Move

On your next project, review the strengths and weaknesses of the different structures, substructures and signposting options we have outlined.

Using the storyboarding technique, experiment with which story structure works best. *Say it out loud:* listen to how well the presentation flows. Ask yourself whether the story is answering the business question - and check how comfortable you feel moving from one point to the next.

Decide on your presentation structure. Select the most compelling story structure options open to you to communicate your storyline. It is now a case of *pick a horse and ride it.* Having made your selection, make sure this structure works - do not keep making last minute changes.

SUMMARY

The aim of the *Structure Tool* is to reinforce the importance of crafting a story where the evidence is integrated and woven together to answer the business question.

A compelling structure will effortlessly lead the audience through the decision choices open to them. There are different structures available to achieve this.

The *linear structure* approach is a simple way of thinking about organising your material.

- ¤ Background/Confrontation/Resolution
- ¤ Challenge/Resolution/Call-to-Action
- ¤ Situation/Complexity/Resolution (Q&A)

The *nonlinear structure* requires a big idea, core concept or killer statistics to sit at the heart of your presentation, around which you then address different perspectives.

¤ **High Level Concept**

¤ **Lead/Support/Tail**

¤ **Interactive Structure**

When you have decided on your overall structure, you can embellish the way you present your story by using *substructures*.

¤ **The Time Machine**

¤ **The Parallel Universe**

¤ **The Comparison**

¤ **The Counterpoint Story**

¤ **The Reverse Story**

You can also use various techniques for *signposting* the overall architecture of the presentation. This will help indicate where you are in the story running order and to highlight different features of the presentation.

Use the *storyboard* technique to experiment with the best story flow.

Next, we look at the *Narrative Tool*. This is about ensuring that your presentation has a distinctive theme that will help reinforce your message.

13 THE NARRATIVE TOOL
How to develop a theme with powerful supporting words to drive your story

The aim of the *Narrative Tool* is to *frame* the way the audience receives your presentation. It seeks to *prime* the audience and focus expectations. This includes developing a *theme* for your presentation together with supporting words that touch the audience's world. The creation of a theme and precision over the words you use will make it easier to communicate your story.

GUIDING PRINCIPLES

Principle One: Ensure your story has a theme that sets the scene

Set up your presentation by ensuring it has a theme that frames - introduces - your core storyline. This will help stakeholders who may be apprehensive about what to expect from your presentation. It will signal whether the findings will suddenly present them with a major problem or be outlining an exciting opportunity.

Principle Two: Respect and take care with words - words have power

As a storyteller, you should enjoy working with words - making sure you have chosen the right words to convey your *exact* meaning. Care with your choice of words throughout your presentation will help you land your message.

Principle Three: Make sure your words, images and data work together to tell the story

Ensure your words work in conjunction with your visuals and the killer evidence. Try to use an image that could be a metaphor for the words you are using and/or data you are presenting.

KEY ACTIONS

Action 1: Develop a theme for your presentation that frames the presentation

Introduce your presentation with a core theme. This framing - priming - will mean your audience will be in the right register to *receive* your presentation.

If, for example, you prime the audience upfront that you are going to present *exciting opportunities*, then they can relax into your presentation. From the outset they can concentrate without getting anxious or concerned.

Intelligent framing - having a theme - will also set the scene for unfolding a bad news story. They will be prepared.

Below is a summary of some key presentation themes. This is not an exhaustive list, but it will give you theme ideas for your narrative. For each category of themes, we have provided some illustrative vocabulary. In creating your slides, it can be helpful to use these kinds of words to reinforce your theme. It will give your presentation a feeling of consistency.

Positive good news themes

Opportunity - opportunities to build for the future: seize, unique, frontier, gold mine, prospect, narrow window.

Evolution - gradual progression: survival of fittest, adapt, survive, natural selection, environment.

Revolution - radical, different changes: uprising, overthrow, rebellion, new wave, authority, take charge.

Challenging themes

Challenge - requires challenging solutions: duel, combat, heroes, hurdles, persistence, preparation, dedication.

Crossroads - deciding whether to go in one of two directions: alternative futures, definite choices, decisive moments, different directions.

Crisis - a very difficult situation: emergency, urgent response, prioritise resources, immediate action, remaining calm.

Survival – overcoming threats and obstacles: extreme environments, overcoming barriers, ingenuity, inner strengths, focus, big changes needed.

Specific scenario themes

Quest - an adventurous programme to achieve a goal: heroes, the great journey, magic, the prize.

The great dream - a big picture vision for the future: vision, epiphany, higher order insight, beacon, raise the bar, fresh perspectives.

Adventure - embarking on a new venture: journey, voyage, embarking, set sail, fun.

Rescue - an initiative to save a situation from becoming worse: obstacles, ingenuity, courage, race against time.

Blow the whistle - highlighting what has not been previously made explicit: reveal, expose, announce, unfold, clarify, bust myths.

Action 2: Ensure your presentation contains a mix of communications styles

Ensuring your evidence is in the right communications register for the audience.

A mix of visual, auditory and kinaesthetic cues

Ensure your presentation is sympathetic to the dominant ways in which people like to receive information.

The rational and emotional perspectives

Get your message over using the right blend of more *emotional* based (System 1) evidence and more *rational* (System 2) evidence.

Action 3: Provide a blend of ideas, powerful concepts and practical examples

We have established that a typical audience will include a mix of those looking for big ideas and those seeking more practical guidance. Therefore, a presentation narrative needs to provide a combination of ideas and practical next steps the audience can take.

Action 4: Reflect on the language you will use in the presentation

Choosing words that give your meaning maximum clarity should not be seen as a chore or as pedantry. Attention to detail with words is critical to your success as a presenter. It is often said that *words are all we have*.

Touch their world

Use concepts, principles and terminology to which the audience can relate. As explained, if you are talking to finance experts, use the language of money. For human resources professionals, reflect their terminology - employee wellbeing. For marketing teams, talk customer sales.

Create a hook

A memorable communications *hook* can take your presentation to the next level. For example, Ronseal's *It Does Exactly What It Says on the Tin* slogan has been at the heart of the company's communications strategy for several decades and is the way the company is remembered.

Clarity

Ensure you explain important detailed complexity. For example, if you are assessing financial literacy in the UK, and exploring awareness of the *Bank Rate*, you need to clarify the difference between the rate set by the Bank of England and the lending rate charged by a High Street Bank.

Accuracy

Be *precise*. For example, you cannot say *more* British than US citizens hold a passport if in fact this is not true in terms of *absolute* numbers. What you really mean is that *proportionally* more British than US citizens hold passports.

Comprehension

Ambiguity is a big enemy to comprehension - the different ways phrases are interpreted. For example, in an immigration survey, participants were asked *How long was your residence in Australia?* The answer 15 metres is not quite what was expected!

Language

Beware of *language leaks* - loose phrases or pejorative wording that can betray a lack of objectivity. For example, there will be differences in the images conjured up by each of the following descriptions of people over 65: *old age pensioners; the elderly; the retired; older people; senior citizens; baby boomers;* and *Silver Surfers.*

Action 5: Apply the Rule of Three: ensure your headline, visuals and evidence work together

Applying the *Rule of Three* ensures that you have an *active* headline, a powerful image (ideally a visual metaphor) and a piece of killer evidence.

Make sure your slide headlines tell your story

Drive your story forward by using *active* headlines. Do not to use bland, stock, loose, *passive* or vague words that tell us nothing.

If you use active words you will create a headline for each presentation slide that tells its own story and, slide by slide, drives home your message. By an *active* headline we mean one that will tell the story of the slide - not just passive descriptive words that do not tell us anything.

Passive headline: Levels of participation in sport in the UK 2012 to 2019.

Active headline: Participation in UK sport has fallen since the 2012 Olympics.

Select powerful visual metaphors to support your storyline

If you make a point with an image, there is a much higher chance that it will be remembered. The recall of a statistic with an image is higher than when the same point is made without the image.

Use an image that is not only engaging but could also be a *metaphor* for what you are trying to say. This, as illustrated below, massively improves the chances of your message registering with the audience.

Child obesity has doubled in five years!

Focus on the killer evidence

Show only the killer evidence to support the headline and main point - remember the principle of telling your story with only 20% of the evidence.

Action 6: Review how the headline, image and evidence work together

Once you have applied the *Rule of Three* to each slide, review the impact this slide is making. How the headline, image and evidence is working together to convey your narrative then refine for maximum effect.

The Rule of Three in action

Let's look at how you would tell the story of the changing nature of the labour market. We start with a data-heavy approach. We then improve this by applying the *Rule of Three*. (This is illustrative data only.)

Text-heavy slide with passive title that fails to tell the story

A review of key trends in the structure of the labour market

- There has been a 21% increase in those working on zero contract hours in the last 12 months

- 51% of the workforce estimated to be in the *gig* economy by 2033

- 45% of millennials report wanting to work for themselves

The Compendium of National Employment Statistics: Detailed analysis of key trends

Active slide title that tells the story

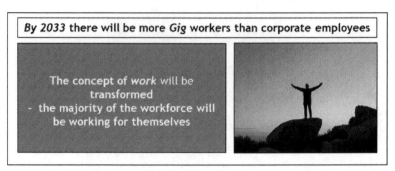

FREQUENTLY ASKED QUESTIONS

Question One: Can some presentations have a mixture of different themes?

Answer: Yes. For example, you may have a positive *opportunity* theme that you may wish to embellish by also talking about the *adventure* of embarking on a new strategy. However, you do *not* want a mix of contradictory themes, drawn from the *positive* <u>and</u> *challenging* ends of the theme spectrum. This works against the whole idea of providing a unifying theme.

Question Two: Is it possible to sustain the *Rule of Three* approach consistently across *all* the slides of a presentation?

Answer: There is an enormous benefit to applying the *Rule of Three* to every slide. By having an active headline, eye-catching image and killer evidence on each slide the audience can work out the storyline, even without the presenter's commentary.

Question Three: How do you explain critical, technical and methodological points in an accessible, jargon-free way?

Answer: It is helpful to *ladder up* to the fundamental concept underpinning a techniques, rather than delving into technicalities of how the method works. For example, at a conceptual level statistical correlation can simply be explained as a technique that examines the *extent and nature of the relationship between different variables.*

Top Tip

Ask someone who knows nothing about your presentation to read out just the headlines to your slides. Then ask them to tell you in a few words what they think the presentation is telling the audience. See how close their answer is to the message you are trying to convey. Then tweak and modify your presentation accordingly.

 Best Next Move

On your next project, review the theme ideas outlined above and select the one that best reflects your presentation. Identify between six and twelve key words you can use to reinforce this theme. Use Roget's Thesaurus! Experiment with different words and phrases that you can use within this theme to give your presentation a coherent feel.

SUMMARY

The Narrative Tool tells us that great presentations benefit from having a theme. We have outlined the following themes:

Positive good news themes - essentially upbeat narratives

- ¤ **Opportunity**
- ¤ **Evolution**
- ¤ **Revolution**

Challenging themes - where there are issues (including bad news) to present to the audience.

- ¤ **Challenge**
- ¤ **Crossroads**
- ¤ **Crisis**
- ¤ **Survival**

Specific scenario themes - to deal with various business situations.

- ¤ **Quest**
- ¤ **The great dream**

¤ **Adventure**

¤ **Rescue**

¤ **Blow the whistle**

Support your theme with an inspired and intelligent choice of words that will engage your audience.

Touch your audience's world with a blend of communications styles.

Make sure you have the right mix of big ideas and practical examples.

Employ the *Rule of Three* technique to ensure your words, images and evidence reinforce each other. Each slide should have an active headline, supported by an eye-catching visual metaphor, together with the killer evidence that best substantiates the point.

Next, we look at the *Impact Tool* - ways of bringing your presentation alive.

14 THE IMPACT TOOL
How to bring your presentation alive and make it stand out

Find the time to polish your presentation to maximise the chances of making a big impact with your audience. The *Impact Tool* is about creating a presentation that has the *wow* factor that keeps the audience engaged from start to finish.

GUIDING PRINCIPLES

Principle One: Engage with your audience at three levels - Thinking, Feeling and Involvement

Think: You need to get your audience to think about your message.

Feel: You need to tap into the way the audience feels about your message.

Involve: Involve the audience through questions - get them to relate what you are saying to their own experiences. This will mean that the audience is more likely to take action based on what you are saying and to share your message with other stakeholders.

Principle Two: Ensure lean-in at critical moments in your presentation

A great presentation will grab everyone's attention at the start. It will also use *lean-in* techniques to (re)energise the audience during the presentation. And it will conclude by leaving a lasting impression.

Principle Three: Create a story - a script - that makes it easy for stakeholders to share with others

Crafting a message that will *stick* and can easily be shared with others is a key communications goal - particularly in our social media world. By creating an easy to repeat *soundbite,* you substantially push up the chances of your audience passing on your message to others. This then becomes a kind of *script* to which everyone becomes aligned. This will help to obtain buy-in to your message.

KEY ACTIONS

Action 1: Change the focus and pace of your presentation to sustain engagement

Below are some impact techniques to help you create impact and retain interest and change the focus and/or pace of your delivery. Steve Jobs made a point of changing the pace of a presentation every ten minutes or so.

The Hero's Tale

Tell your story through the eyes of an individual. This changes the pace from presenting *aggregate statistics* to looking at the topic through the *lens of an individual*. (This could be a modal customer or a character at the centre of the point you wish to illustrate.)

This technique is one that film directors have deployed for many years. They take a major event and making it accessible by explaining their story through the eyes of an individual. An example is the film about the D-Day landings. This epic event is told through the lens of an individual soldier, hence the film title: *Saving Private Ryan*.

This approach is also now commonplace in news reporting. Over the years we have seen a shift in the way that major news stories are told. Several decades ago, the BBC News, in reporting a war, would focus its coverage on the key macro geo-political factors in play. But today, the BBC also tells stories about conflicts through the eyes of an individual solider or civilian.

The Deep Dive

Another technique to engage the audience is the deep dive. Put the spotlight on a key issue and explore this in greater detail than other topics.

For example, as part of a presentation on customer satisfaction, provide details of a frequent customer complaint. Illustrate this with a recorded account of a conversation between an irate customer and the client's Customer Complaints Manager.

Inspirational success stories

Another powerful lean-in technique is to explain how a successful market leader or big-name brand might have handled a similar situation. This is an excellent way of changing the pace, grabbing attention and re-energising the audience. Talking about the success of key competitors is guaranteed to focus stakeholders on what they need to do to keep up.

For example, you could showcase an online retailer renowned for excellence and take the audience through all the *customer touchpoints* in its purchasing journey - highlighting how they excel.

Action 2: Bring in your own point of view

As the presenter you should demonstrate presence. Be the person who raises the temperature in the room. Be enthusiastic, inspirational and empathise with stakeholders. Insight professionals are *admissible evidence*: it is expected that they have a point of view, add value and do not remain neutral. To deliver this, build into your presentation moments where you will offer your own informed point of view. Introduce the *personal storytelling* technique.

Personal Storytelling episodes

Personal storytelling episodes give you an opportunity to explain how the evidence fits with your overall experience. It is legitimate to share your own personal views about an aspect of the research process or business challenge - provide your *take* on events. It is important to stress that these interventions must remain business-like and credible. This is *not* an invitation to tell obscure, self-indulgent, self-referential anecdotes.

For example, you might want to explain how you felt about powerful comments being made in the focus groups you conducted. Or you may want to contextualise a compelling piece of quantitative evidence by sharing how you felt when you first learnt about this.

These personal storytelling episodes - interventions - need to be carefully selected and positioned in your presentation. As you develop the craft of storytelling, you will be able to deliver these on a more spontaneous basis.

167

Action 3: Make sure you involve the audience

Another way of gaining impact is to make sure that you involve the audience.

Ask the audience questions

The simplest involvement technique is simply to ask questions at critical points in the presentation. This will ensure that you are not *lecturing* the audience, but instead creating a two-way dialogue.

The first point at which you might introduce a question could be after around five minutes. Use this to test the mood of the audience to see how well you are being received.

For example, after presenting a key statistic, you could ask if this is a pattern or trend the audience recognises. Then after presenting a key finding, you could ask if this is new or surprising - or something they were expecting. And towards the end of the presentation, you could ask if there is an action that they could now take, based on what you are saying.

Self-assessment

Another powerful lean-in technique is to encourage the audience to undertake some self-assessment of their position. For example, you could say, *Hands up those who have experienced what I have just said about X?*

Audience participation

Involve the audience by encouraging participation in an *activity*. For example, get the audience to access a competitor website or ask them to examine the quality of the packaging for a new product.

The Myth Buster

Introduce an element of surprise by debunking received wisdom and challenging cherished beliefs or myths. This is a good way of involving the audience. For example, a hotel may believe that it offers world-class customer service. But in reality, it is inflexible. Call out the fact that it struggles when customers request something that falls outside the hotel's standard systems and processes.

Future Histories

Another technique to get involvement is to paint vivid pictures of what is likely to happen in the future if stakeholders do *not* take action now. Painting *future histories* - imagining the future - and outlining the action needed is a powerful way of getting conversations started.

Action 4: Prepare your strategy for answering stakeholder questions

In the *Insight Story Builder,* we are not focusing on presentation delivery, but it is helpful to highlight some techniques to help you manage the presentation on the day and make an impact. It is important that you do not let your presentation be ruined by failing to anticipate questions that could disrupt you on the day. It is all about expecting the unexpected and being prepared: *All the best ad lib lines are well rehearsed!*

Be authoritative

Be completely clear about what questions you *must* know the answers to on the day in order to maintain credibility. For example, if you are giving a presentation on how to improve a business magazine, you must know how many people read the publication. But it would be acceptable for you not to know how many readers responded to a specific promotion run by the magazine two years ago.

Be succinct, concise and concrete

Provide succinct and concise answers to questions. You should provide direct, concrete answers, without abstract theorising or frustrating qualifications. But, do not trivialise or oversimplify your point. In addition, be supportive of the person asking the question - do not make them feel that their question was obtuse or ill-informed.

Demonstrate business acumen

One resistance to *market research* is the perception that it is too academic. So, in answering questions, demonstrate a strong business presence. Register the fact that you understand stakeholders' complex decision-making world. You are not just a methodological expert. Senior stakeholders welcome consultants who can take the helicopter view - see the big picture - and identify the key business concepts in play. Here it is helpful to use business heuristics - rules of thumb - that apply to the business question.

Avoid diffident market research language

In answering questions, avoid *hesitant* market research language. Market research has evolved using language designed to explain the risk and uncertainty associated with sample survey evidence: sampling error, margin of error, confidence limits and so on. But in today's fast-moving soundbite culture, these respectable methodological research terms can suggest that the presenter is unsure and lacks conviction about what they are saying. Be confident and assertive in your tone and manner.

Avoid methodological jargon

It is easy to slip into jargon that is familiar to insight professionals, but puzzling for those not steeped in the methodological world. For example, in conveying the *validity* and *reliability* of your evidence, do not get bogged down with technical definitions. Instead, you could say that you believe that your observation about X would not fundamentally change if the survey was repeated.

It is also helpful to move away from the language of statistical significance to the holistic language we suggested in the Holistic Frame. Borrow from the lawyer's lexicon and talk about the *safety of the evidence.*

Action 5: Get stakeholder engagement with your presentation

Promote your upcoming presentation to stakeholders. For example, give careful thought to creating an impactful *subject title* to your email telling them about your presentation. This subject title should prompt the reader to open the email to find out more.

You could also use innovative tactics to involve stakeholders who could not attend the presentation. Why not send out a short video capturing the key points.

Also find ways of engaging a wider audience with your key findings. You could try *gamification* - set up a *quiz*. For example, send out a communication centred on your presentation that says, *Do you know the profile of the grocery customers who spend more than £150 a week with you?*

Action 6: Communicate insights on a rolling basis

Increasingly, the emphasis is on providing *rolling* communications rather than everything hinging on one final presentation. So, make sure you keep stakeholders involved with the key insights at critical touchpoints during the project. This *priming* and *framing* will help with your delivery of the final presentation.

FREQUENTLY ASKED QUESTIONS

Question One: Should Impact Tool techniques be structured into the presentation or can they be used on a more spontaneous basis depending on how the presentation is going?

Answer: The general advice would be to factor into your presentation three Impact Tools. *Start* with an impact technique that gives extra edge at the beginning to engage and focus the audience. Use another Impact Tool *midway* through your presentation to obtain lean-in and keep the audience energised. Then, introduce another technique at the *end* to make sure you leave the audience with a clear picture of what action you want them to take.

These could be *plumbed* into the presentation to grab attention, sustain engagement and leave a lasting impression. In addition, an experienced presenter will also have in their *back pocket* one or two personal storytelling episodes that they may use depending on how the presentation is going.

Question Two: With regard to involving the audience, by asking them questions, is there a danger that this can disturb the overall flow of the presentation?

Answer: If you have a presentation with no opportunities to involve the audience, you keep control, but it could come over as a lecture - a tiresome monologue. But equally, if there is too much audience involvement the presenter can lose control of the presentation. They might not even get to deliver their message because the session deteriorates into a free-for-all questions fest.

It is about managing the situation and applying judgement. If you are giving a 30-minute presentation it would seem sensible to build in - after around 10 and then 20-minutes - an interlude to get feedback from the audience. Then you can play it by ear about how many further times during the presentation you might want to involve the audience.

Question Three: Just how far should you go in offering your own personal point of view - not remaining neutral?

Answer: Today, an audience expects the insight professional to have a point of view. However, this is *not* an invitation to express an entirely personal viewpoint unrelated to the evidence. Your opinion should be firmly evidence based. So, let's say you have framed three decision options. It is entirely legitimate to review the case for and against each option and then - based on your judgement and the evidence - to suggest the option that would be your own preferred route.

 Top Tip

Involve a *critical friend* who will roleplay being the *client from hell* to go through a dry run of your presentation and ask deliberately challenging questions. Use this feedback to make decisions about where you may need to reframe key points using Impact Tool techniques.

 Best Next Move

On your next project, identify the Impact Tools that you can plumb into the structure of your presentation in order to touch the world of your audience at the *beginning, middle* and *end* of your presentation. Craft personal storytelling episodes you could possibly introduce to reinforce your message. Anticipate the most demanding and challenging questions that could be asked in the presentation and prepare how you will answer these. Finally, it is helpful to ask yourself three questions:

- ¤ Have I answered the *business question* - the issue that is at the core of this presentation?
- ¤ Has there been a complete understanding of the key *Message* I am delivering to the audience?

¤ Have I achieved my *Purpose* - have I brought about the change in the audience I intended?

If there is any doubt about your success in achieving the above aims, then revisit each of the seven Story Tools to identify ways of ensuring that the key goals have been achieved.

SUMMARY

The Impact Tool is designed to bring your presentation alive and make it stand out.

Use impact techniques to help you change the focus and pace of the presentation. These could include:

¤ **Hero's Tale**

¤ **Deep Dive**

¤ **Inspirational Success Stories**

¤ **Personal storytelling episodes**

Use techniques for involving the audience to ensure the presentation is not a monologue but one that engages and involves the audience and is interactive. Techniques to consider:

¤ **Ask the audience questions**

¤ **Self-assessment**

¤ **Audience participation**

¤ **The Myth Buster**

¤ **Future Histories**

Make sure you can handle stakeholder questions.

Sell your presentation to stakeholders and make it easy for those who may not have been able to attend your presentation to access your findings. Release findings on a rolling basis.

To conclude Part Two, we bring together the *Seven Story Tools* into the *Story Builder Framework* to help you create a compelling storyline.

The Story Builder Framework

We conclude this part of the book by drawing together the Seven Story Tools into our Story Builder Framework. This process is outlined below:

Review each of the Story Tools

Audience Tool: Have you met the audience's expectations?

Purpose Tool: Have you done everything possible to achieve your purpose?

Message Tool: Is your message concise, clear and memorable?

Evidence Tool: Have you reduced the data down to the killer evidence?

Structure Tool: Have you employed an elegant, easy to follow structure?

Narrative Tool: Do you have a distinctive theme and flowing narrative?

Impact Tool: Have you used impact techniques to keep the audience engaged?

Enter your key observations into the Story Builder Framework

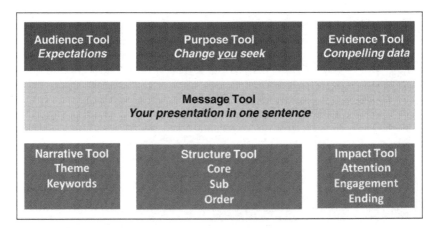

Prepare slide headlines

Take the overall structure and begin to draft the headlines of the key slides that fall under each of the main categories in your presentation. Below we use the illustration of the *Background/Confrontation/Resolution* structure template.

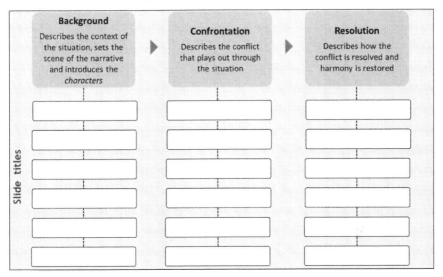

The final step in this process is to do the *look and speak test* using the slides. By looking at the slide titles, work through and see how your narrative works. Check how well it flows using this particular structure and these slide titles?

In Part Three we look at strategies for turning *Insights into Action.*

PART THREE

INSIGHTS INTO ACTION

How to make sure customer
insights are actioned

Insights into Action

Customer insight is one of the most valuable assets any organisation possesses. But often powerful insights fall by the wayside. In Part Three we focus on building the customer insight professional's capability to influence, persuade and ensure action is taken to implement the insights they have presented.

Consultancy Strategies for turning insights into action

We look at overcoming the different resistances that stand in the way of the insight professional successfully persuading stakeholders to take action. We provide various strategies for overcoming barriers to the successful implementation of your insight message.

Insights into Action

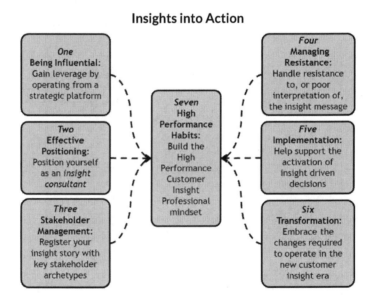

How we explain each Strategy

We start by outlining the *Guiding Principles* underpinning the strategy. We follow this with *Key Actions* to apply this strategy. Next are some *Frequently Asked Questions*. We follow this with a *Top Tip*. Then there is your *Best Next Move* - ideas on applying the strategy to your next project. We conclude with a *Summary*.

We start by looking at operating from an *Influential* strategic platform.

15 BEING INFLUENTIAL
How to gain leverage by operating from a strategic platform

Turning insights into action begins with ensuring the customer insight team gains leverage by operating from an influential platform within the organisation. You will enhance the chances of driving home an insight message if the insight function has successfully built a reputation for adding value and being at the heart of shaping future strategy.

GUIDING PRINCIPLES

Principle One: Establish the insight team as value creators

The customer insight team should not be seen as a reactive order-taking function responding to day-to-day tactical issues. Build your credibility as a group of trusted insight consultants who create value. Do not allow the team to get positioned as technicians who are just dealing with day-to-day issues.

Principle Two: Focus the insight team on futureproofing the organisation

The insight team needs to build a reputation for being experts in *futureproofing* the organisation. The ability to turn a specific insight message into action will be dramatically enhanced if the insight function has built a reputation for being proactive in driving the organisation's change agenda.

Principle Three: Build the reputation of the insight team as the go-to customer centricity experts

The likelihood of your insight message being received, and acted upon, will be improved if you have driven home the credentials of the customer insight team as experts in customer centric decision-making. It is important to *socialise* your insight success stories. Make sure the customer insights you are providing are disseminated to key stakeholders throughout the organisation.

KEY ACTIONS

Action 1: Build the insight team's credibility as co-creators of insight

The insight team needs to work in collaboration with stakeholders in co-creating insights. Insights are not miraculously *found* in the data but *created* in a strategic dialogue between the insight team and senior management. This requires insight professionals to be the experts in interpreting the customer and market evidence. But they must also have the business acumen to identify actionable insights capable of driving growth and profitability. The team needs to showcase its role in creating value into the future.

Action 2: Make seizing opportunities the core of the insight team's role

Increasingly, the focus will be on identifying strategic foresights that help organisations manage the change agenda. This requires the customer insight team to build a reputation for seizing strategic opportunities in a timely way. There are massive dividends in establishing the team's credentials as experts in *futureproofing* the organisation - equipping it to deal with disruption and change.

Building on this, the insight team should take responsibility for creating a *learning organisation.* Insight needs to be at the centre of an agile customer centric culture that seamlessly adapts to change on a rolling basis. The team should be the *gurus* when it comes to synthesising multiple sources of evidence into an integrated narrative that informs the organisation's strategic thinking.

Action 3: Align the insight team with the customer centricity agenda

Being customer centric as an organisation is good for business: organisational growth and profitability flows from being committed to being truly customer centric. The customer insight team needs to leverage this reality. It is important to build the team's reputation as the individuals - *insight champions* - within the organisation who most understand the customer. This will create an authoritative platform on which to build when influencing and persuading stakeholders on a specific insight project.

Action 4: Ensure the insight team has a line of sight to the C-Suite

Establish the customer insight team's credentials as a trusted strategic partner who has access to the C-Suite. If you are operating in the back room, you are not going to be able to turn insights into action. Your access to the C-Suite will demonstrate that you are aware of the organisation's business vision and future strategy.

It will mean you are well placed to ensure customer insights inform business thinking and are driving the prevailing strategy of the organisation. It will also encourage C-Suite members and other senior managers to become allies: they can help you disseminate the insight story throughout the organisation.

Action 5: Build the customer insight team's reputation by socialising insight success stories

Stakeholders who see the success of your last insight will be more readily disposed to respond positively to your next insight message. So, take personal responsibility for communicating the value of the insight function throughout the organisation. Build the team's reputation for being in the results business.

Demonstrate the overall value of insight by regularly disseminating compelling insight stories and case studies throughout the whole organisation.

Think about using innovative communications techniques, such as short videos, to constantly put the value of insight in front of senior stakeholders.

Action 6: Ensure the customer insight team is in the vanguard of the digital transformation of insight

Ensure the insight team leads the way in how to use digital, Artificial Intelligence (AI) and Machine Learning (ML) generated insights as part of the mix in imagining the future and creating powerful strategic insights. Demonstrate mastery in interpreting insights *generated* by AI and ML sources.

Of all the professionals working in the AI/ML space, customer insight professionals are arguably the best equipped to make sense of AI/ML outputs because they have the (psychological) understanding of the customer. It is insight professionals who know how to ask the critical *why* questions and apply wisdom and judgement to obtain the optimum solution.

FREQUENTLY ASKED QUESTIONS

Question One: Surely it would be safer for customer insight professionals to just focus on advising on tactical studies rather than them attempting to be influential around big, strategic futureproofing initiatives?

> **Answer:** It may be safer to focus on the small stuff but, to gain a reputation as a trusted advisor, customer insight professionals need to operate in the strategic futureproofing space. They need to be in the vanguard of helping organisations cope with disruption and to seize opportunities in a timely way.

Question Two: What if you sense senior management do not believe that being customer centric is a key driver of growth and profitability?

> **Answer:** Showcase - on a project-by-project basis - the way insights in consumer behaviour have led to profitable outcomes for the organisation. Demonstrate the advantages customer centric organisations enjoy over those that do not prioritise customer centricity. Do this through a constant flow of insight success case stories about the power of customer insight.

Question Three: How do customer insight professionals remain influential and differentiate themselves in the customer centricity space in the face of competition from data scientists, management consultants and others?

> **Answer:** Customer insight professionals have the edge over others working in the insight space because they are experts in customer behaviour. They understand *why* customers make particular decisions. They know what makes customers *tick*. This is the key pillar in building their reputation and influence.

Top Tip

Build the team's reputation for identifying strategic opportunities. Establish the insight team's capability in taking the *helicopter view* of what is happening in the business. Do not just react to tactical requests for information that come your way. Be the expert in scanning the business radar for big disruptors. Take personal responsibility for waving the red flag if you feel these present any danger.

>>> Best Next Move

As a member of the customer insight team, score your own team on each of the following criteria. Use a scale where 10 means the team is doing extremely well and 1 means there is room for improvement.

- ¤ Building a reputation for being proactive in identifying strategic opportunities - going beyond taking the market research order.
- ¤ Establishing a reputation for playing a strategic futureproofing role.
- ¤ Being recognised as being at the heart of driving customer centric change.
- ¤ Securing a line of sight to the C-Suite so that the team is aware of the organisation's business vision and future strategy.
- ¤ Building a reputation for *socialising* the power of customer insight.
- ¤ Being at the leading edge of demonstrating how to blend AI and ML generated insights into the insight generation process?

Focus on those areas where you have only awarded the team a low score and make this a priority for improvement.

SUMMARY

Ensure the customer insight team is recognised as being at the heart of driving the customer centricity agenda. The insight team needs to play a pivotal role in working with senior stakeholders in the co-creation of insight.

Reinforce the team's credentials as being at the centre of *futureproofing* the organisation.

The customer insight team needs to establish a clear line of sight to the C-Suite. It also needs to regularly demonstrate the success of the insight function by disseminating - *socialising* - insight success stories.

The customer insight team should be in the vanguard of the digital transformation of insight - demonstrating that their understanding of customers is essentially interpreting the outputs from AI/ML.

In the next chapter we look at the most *Effective Positioning* for the individual insight professional working within an insight team.

16 EFFECTIVE POSITIONING
How to position yourself as an insight consultant

We have examined the platform from which the customer insight function should operate in order to leverage insights within the organisation. We now turn to the *stance* the individual customer insight professional should adopt to maximise their effectiveness in dealing with stakeholders.

GUIDING PRINCIPLES

Principle One: Position yourself as framing the decision choices

Operate as an evidence-based consultant who is framing the decision choices open to stakeholders. Do not get into the position of being in the hot seat of having to conjure up a specific yes/no style recommendation. Instead, adopt a stance that takes the stakeholder through - in a consultative way - the prior thinking you have followed in constructing the eventual recommendation.

Principle Two: Position yourself as driving the strategic direction of the organisation

Position yourself as a consultant with the skillset to identify themes and trends that alert the organisation to possible disruption, and help it seize key business opportunities. Go beyond advising at a tactical level on an individual project-by-project basis by demonstrating how insights can be used to drive the growth and profitability of the organisation.

Principle Three: Position yourself as an expert in insight driven business solutions

Position yourself as an expert in knowing precisely how powerful insights can influence customer behaviour when addressing critical business challenges.

KEY ACTIONS

Action 1: Operate from an authoritative consultative stance

The stance from which you deliver your insights is critical. Some insight consultants seem to have been manoeuvred into operating from a fundamentally flawed consultative stance - position. They make the mistake of allowing themselves to be cajoled into operating from the highly vulnerable position of having to provide futureproof recommendations and predictions without the full knowledge of the business context.

They get lured into the role of being some kind of *magician* with a crystal ball who is expected to pull a rabbit out of the hat - an insight - in order to answer the business question. It is vital not to get pigeon-holed into the almost impossible to deliver role of the *fortune teller* with an insight-based recommendation for the audience.

Below is a step-by-step process for ensuring the insight consultant is operating from a position that will play to their strengths as an evidence-based insight consultant. This avoids being positioned as some kind of pundit who somehow arrives at a conclusion.

Frame the decision choices for the decision-maker

It is important to position yourself as the consultant *framing* the decision choices for stakeholders.

For each of the decision choices you have framed, identify the available opportunities

The next step is to identify the *opportunities* that each decision choice offers, including providing the killer evidence showcasing what success looks like.

Identify the risks associated with each prioritised option

Next identify the *risks* associated with each of the prioritised options, again providing the killer evidence to paint a picture of exactly what the risk looks like in pursuing this option.

Assess the likelihood of success of each prioritised option

For each decision option, assess the *likelihood of success* for this option. This could, for example, include applying game theory about how competitors might react to the different solutions being considered.

In making a judgement on the likelihood of success, it is helpful to take account of the opportunities you have with this option for course correction en route. If you sense you have made broadly the right decision, and also know that you can adjust this decision later in the process, then this pushes up the probability of success. Success is more difficult to achieve when you are locked into a decision and have little room for manoeuvre after the decision is made.

Consequences: Looking at the wider context and future implications

An effective positioning - stance - will include outlining the wider and longer-term strategic foresights and implications related to a particular decision. In the new customer insight paradigm, the emphasis is on spotting and seizing opportunities for growth. It is about *futureproofing* the organisation. Highly effective customer insight professionals will put this at the heart of their consultative role.

Set up a Decision Assessment Framework

The next step in getting your consultative positioning right involves providing an assessment of each of the prioritised framed decision outcomes to help stakeholders arrive at their optimum decision. It is helpful to set up a *Decision Assessment Framework*. This summarises the evidence in favour of, and also against, each of the decision options. It means that you can see at a glance how the evidence is building to support each particular option.

Providing a recommendation

Stakeholders may or may not invite the consultant to provide a recommendation on the final decision to be taken. The good news is that, if you are called to give your opinion, you are now operating from a position of authority and strength.

You will have *framed* the choices, evaluated the evidence around *opportunities* and *risks*, assessed the *likelihood of success*, and also examined the wider *consequences.* These steps will help pave the way for making a *recommendation* that will then come across as professional and informed by the business strategy.

Action 2: Demonstrate your expertise in the power of customer insight

Claim the territory of the insight expert. Position yourself as the professional who really understands how to influence consumer behaviour. This starts with having total clarity in your own mind about what does, and does not, pass muster as a *genuine* commercially scalable customer insight capable of changing consumer behaviour.

Know what an insight is!

To be an influential consultant you need to establish yourself as an *insight guru* who knows what a true insight is - which insights have the power to change consumer behaviour. We have established that a true insight has a *psychological* and *behavioural* dimension. It should tell us about consumers' core motivations and how these affect their behaviour.

We have also explained that insights are rarely *found*. Insights are *created* out of the data in a *fierce* intellectual dialogue between the insight professional and the project stakeholders.

Understand the power of your insight - how your insight might work to change consumer behaviour

Getting to the heart of how an insight works

The following questions will help establish the robustness of the insight that is the nub of the presentation. These will help you identify whether or not you have a genuine insight that will drive and change behaviour.

- ¤ Does this *insight* pivot around what you have learnt about what the customer believes to be true but isn't? Addressing this misconception would be the key part of your storyline.
- ¤ Does this *insight* tell us something about what customers do not yet realise but, if they did realise it, then this would cause them to move

to a new solution? If so, this is the dimension that would lie at the heart of your storyline.

¤ Does this *insight* allow us to crystallise something in the mind of customers that, when this has cascaded through their belief (thinking) and feeling (emotional system), would ultimately encourage them to realise that your solution is genuinely an innovative answer to their problem? If so, clearly this is a powerful storyline.

¤ Does this *insight* provide us with a specific action that, if you told customers, would immediately produce the *Aha* moment for them: would they change their behaviour and buy into your solution? If so, this would make a compelling storyline.

Crystallise your insight

It is helpful to crystallise in a precise statement how your putative insight will work to encourage the desired change in customer behaviour. This statement needs to encapsulate the essence of the insight. Being able to create a succinct statement that crystallises your insight will help stakeholders evaluate the power of your insight.

Action 3: Showcase your expertise in unearthing strategic foresights

A strong consultative positioning benefits from having the reputation for helping the organisation identify and seize business opportunities - and to wave the red flag to highlight any potential risks.

This futureproofing expertise places the insight professional in the vanguard of what is now critically important to organisations. This is being able to handle disruption and respond quickly to trends that could change their business model.

There is considerable benefit in positioning yourself as the insight professional best able to identify strategic foresights critical to the organisation's future.

Arriving at a strategic foresight has the following specific phases:

- Identify a piece of *data* and begin to link this to other data points.

- Make *observations* about the meaning and implications of different pieces of data.

- Identify the key *themes* that are emerging by looking at how these observations are coming together.

- Identify *trends* that are emerging from these themes.

- Identify new *paradigms* - fundamental changes and shifts in how people are now viewing the world.

- Examine the drivers of this new paradigm - identify *strategic foresights* about customers that allow the business to drive growth and profitability.

When I'm 64!

Below we look at the way a strategic foresight could be built to explore the changes taking place in the labour market and the implications for retirement.

Data: More people are becoming self-employed with fewer corporate jobs being available.

Observation: There is a growing level of dissatisfaction about working in larger corporations, coupled with the emergence of the *gig economy* and portfolio (multiple job) working.

Theme: The role that work, employment and career play in people's lives is changing. Many now seem to define and develop themselves in ways unrelated to work.

Trend: There is an increasing number of millennials and newcomers to the labour market looking for a radically different experience from work. They expect *employee wellbeing* to be on the agenda.

Paradigm shift: We are moving into an era where there is less of a sharp division between what is *play* and what is *work*.

Strategic foresight: This trend is challenging the traditional concept of working up to a set age then retiring. The concept of *retirement* will become much more fluid.

Action 4: Provide powerful customer focused business solutions

Today, there is an expectation that insight professionals will deliver powerful insights capable of changing behaviour and building growth and profitability. You need to position yourself as providing a *business edge.* The strategic insight consultant will focus on helping the organisation ensure that it is *playing where it is most likely to win,* knows *how to win* and *how to get there.*

Establish how the insight will drive the business solution

You need to be crystal clear about how the core unifying idea - fundamental insight - will drive your storyline. The insight professional will have in their armoury a range of forensic questions to interrogate the feasibility (and commercial viability) of the proposed business solution.

- What critical assumptions have been made about how people might respond to this insight-based decision which - if proved to be incorrect - will have the most significant consequences for the way we are proposing to proceed?

- Let's assume the most significant and substantive piece of consumer evidence that is leading us to this insight is wrong. What are the consequences of pursuing our current course of action?

- What are the remaining key unknowns? Work through the various *What Ifs* - different scenarios - and see where this takes the proposed plan of action.

Making things happen

To further build your reputation as a business focused insight consultant make sure that you commit to taking action to *land* the business opportunity.

- Anticipate what might happen to a project in the future and showing high energy in addressing possible scenarios.

- Become the go-to person for sorting an issue (not just assuming that someone else will be dealing with this).

- Be action orientated. Prioritise taking action on big ticket challenges before dealing with *hygiene* factors. (Operate the *90-minute Principle* by ensuring that, for the first 90 minutes of each day, you focus on the critical business issues that need to be addressed.)

Action 5: Build the winning mindset

Position yourself as a consultant with a *growth mindset* who can identify and solve challenges, rather than someone who just raises problems and blocks progress. Operating from the growth (positive) not *fixed* (negative) mindset is about:

- ¤ Embracing, not avoiding, challenges.
- ¤ Persisting in the face of setbacks, not getting defensive or giving up easily.
- ¤ Seeing effort as a path to mastery, not effort as being fruitless.
- ¤ Learning from criticism, not ignoring negative feedback.
- ¤ Finding lessons and inspiration from, and not feeling threatened by, the success of others.
- ¤ Seeing intelligence and capability as something that can be developed, not as being static or fixed.

Action 6: Demonstrate the commercial value - business impact - of your insights

It is important to reinforce your consultative positioning by demonstrating the commercial value - business impact - you are making in your insight role. This is a complex issue, but there are various ways in which this might be achieved.

- ¤ There could be straightforward situations where it is possible to identify a precise business metric that demonstrates an improvement in profit or revenue that can be directly related to an insight-based action.
- ¤ When it is not practicable to identify a precise business metric, it may be possible to identify *surrogate* metrics - such as the number of new customers generated. Use these as a proxy for measuring the business impact of an insight.
- ¤ Where it is difficult to isolate the contribution of customer insight, compared to other factors, produce success case studies. Let stakeholders see the role that insight has played in creating business success.

FREQUENTLY ASKED QUESTIONS

Question One: What are the most important characteristics the insight consultant needs to develop if they are to position themselves as credible, authoritative, trusted advisors with stakeholders?

> **Answer:** Stakeholders can always *smell desperation!* They will recognise a consultant who is not on top of their game, does not fully understand the evidence and has a shaky grasp of the key business issues. To gain credibility and to enjoy the *winner's advantage,* get your consultative positioning right. This will help you build two key consultative traits - confidence and presence.

Question Two: What if there is resistance from stakeholders about an insight consultant adopting the framing and evaluating the choices stance, rather than simply going straight into making a recommendation?

> **Answer:** We are not suggesting that you do not make a recommendation. We are proposing that this follows the process we have outlined for framing the decision options.

Question Three: Is it always necessary to set up a formal *Decision Assessment Framework* in order to deliver your consultative positioning stance?

> **Answer:** Not necessarily: the Decision Assessment Framework can be followed as a thinking process - mental model - the consultant can apply when evaluating the respective strengths of the evidence supporting each decision option.

 Top Tip

> Make sure you are in the driving seat by operating as a strategic consultant and insight expert who is framing the decision choices. Do not set yourself up for a failure by allowing yourself to be boxed into having to conjure up a yes/no recommendation based on limited information about the strategic context to the business issue.

Best Next Move

On your next project, make sure you are operating from an authoritative consultative stance by working through the process outlined for advising stakeholders. This starts by framing the decision choices that are open to the stakeholder. Then for each decision choice, identify the opportunities and risks that each option presented. Follow this with an assessment of the likelihood of success of each option, together with an outline the longer-term consequences of taking this action. At the end of this consultative process, the presenter may then wish to offer a final recommendation.

SUMMARY

Many insight professionals can get their positioning wrong - the stance from which they operate.

They allow themselves to be cajoled into the highly vulnerable position of having to provide recommendations, but without necessarily being privy to the full strategic context of the business issue.

To avoid falling into this trap, adopting the consultative process we outlined will be helpful.

Start by identifying - *framing* - each of the decision choices.

Next, identify the *opportunities* and *risks* associated with each - supplying the appropriate evidence.

Then, make an assessment of the *likelihood of success* of each decision choice.

Follow this by reviewing the *consequences* of each.

Then, only at this point, offer a *recommendation* as to your own preferred choice.

This consultative approach combines data with judgement. It takes away the pressure on the presenter to make a massive leap from the data to offering a point of view.

Successful positioning requires demonstrating your expertise in knowing what constitutes a powerful commercially viable insight-based decision, a thought provoking strategic foresight and a compelling business solution.

It is important to cultivate the growth (not fixed) mindset.

It is important to constantly demonstrate the commercial value of the impact you are making.

Next, we look at *Stakeholder Management* - making sure you are effective in engaging with different types of stakeholder.

17 STAKEHOLDER MANAGEMENT
How to ensure your insight story registers with key stakeholder archetypes

We now look at different strategies to ensure you are engaging with key stakeholders in a way that acknowledges, respects and plays to the strengths of their personality types. This will maximise the chances of your insight message being actioned.

GUIDING PRINCIPLES

Principle One: Take into account the prevailing organisational culture

Put yourself in your stakeholders' shoes and reflect on the organisational culture in which they operate. There will be conventions and practices that need to be respected in different environments. These range from large public sector organisations to small and medium-sized companies. The start point for managing stakeholders begins by demonstrating a sensitivity towards these bigger picture cultural factors.

Principle Two: Be aware of stakeholder approaches to decision-making

Some stakeholders will listen step-by-step to your presentation as you build up to your conclusions and then make a decision at the *end* of the process. But this is not always the case. Sometimes, senior audiences will be making decisions in *real time* during the course of the presentation. They look at a piece of evidence and instantly draw conclusions about what this is telling them.

Principle Three: Tailor your communications style to how stakeholders receive information

It is easy to fall into the trap of only delivering the presentation in a style that suits you as a presenter, rather than taking into account the preferred learning styles of the audience. We know that some people are more *visual*, some are more *auditory*, and others are looking for more *kinaesthetic* practical illustrations.

This is not suggesting that people *exclusively* receive information in each of these ways, but many people do have a dominant mode. Therefore, make sure that your communications style take this into account and provide a mix of visual, auditory and kinaesthetic approaches.

KEY STAKEHOLDER ARCHETYPES

We now look at how to communicate with six fundamental *Stakeholder Archetypes*. For each we provide an overview, review their key characteristics, and provide tips on how to interact with that archetype.

Archetype 1: The Visionary - wants the big picture helicopter view

Overview

- ¤ Wants big ideas, enjoys concepts, is time urgent, wants to understand the context and the key drivers.
- ¤ Enjoys independent thinking and likes to place new ideas into existing theories and begin to form their own new concepts and visions.
- ¤ Enjoys linking ideas to create patterns for the future and is tolerant of complexity and ambiguity when working to achieve this vision.

Characteristics

- ¤ Comfortable with complex strategic issues but can be restless if confronted with too much detail that they see as getting in the way of their bigger ideas. Tends to be creative and enjoy working with a blank sheet of paper.

¤ They are interested in knowing the *why* behind big ideas - and combine this understanding with their own instincts and intuition to make big decisions.

¤ Will largely absorb presentations by listening and reflecting and asking some *why* questions, but not overly interrogative in presentation settings.

How to interact

¤ They are looking for a high level strategic account of the solution to the business question (tactical and operational details can be addressed elsewhere).

¤ Touch their world - use business heuristics and metrics with which they are familiar.

¤ Pass on your message in one sentence - make this short, clear and memorable.

¤ Use simple and impactful slides to communicate with them - don't inundate them with detailed data.

¤ Explain why certain detailed tasks are necessary.

¤ Be inspirational - show how successful companies are tackling this issue.

Archetype 2: The Dominant Personality - suspicious of an expert's facts and believe their own intuitive point of view must be right

Overview

¤ They are not good listeners and do not enjoy taking other people's advice.

¤ They tend to stick to what they have always believed, even in face of compelling insight evidence.

¤ It is difficult to get them to shift their position, even when presented with incontestable evidence.

Characteristics

¤ These dominant personalities take the view that they have succeeded by being suspicious of experts, consultants and market research evidence. They believe that their own intuition and instincts - trusting their own point of view - has been the key to the success they have achieved.

¤ They can be destructive or even hostile to advice if it goes against their own point of view. The idea of making a U-turn is seen as a sign of weakness - it is not seen as being flexible and open to new thinking. This resistance to advice may tap into insecurities they have about their role - they see this as threatening their position.

¤ They could be particularly uncomfortable with qualitative evidence, perceiving this as being rather *flaky* and personalised.

How to interact

¤ Do not be threatening, overly confrontational or take an aggressive stance with these personalities. Try to take a sympathetic, even empathetic, stance. Soak up, listen and relate to this archetype's argument. When you have built some trust, gradually progress to being more assertive.

¤ Encourage this archetype to reflect and review their position. Try techniques such as:

Contextualising: Invite these individuals to review of their position in the context of what colleagues are saying. Position this feedback as being from *peers* not outside experts.

Casting into the future: Paint a picture of what the future would look like if an insight is actioned. Lead this archetype to the belief that they have come to see this future picture for themselves.

Throw them a bone: Offer them a compromise position presented as only a slight shift from what they currently think but in a way that builds alignment with others.

Connections not Alternatives: It makes sense to avoid suddenly presenting a stark new *unannounced alternative* idea to a dominant personality stakeholder. The better approach is to identify in advance those elements of your new idea that could be *connected* to the stakeholder's existing ideas. This will allow you to unfold your new bold idea in a *softly-softly* way, gaining support as you go.

Archetype 3: The Questioner - seeks to understand by questioning and needs examples of ideas in practice

Overview

¤ This archetype arrives at their understanding by asking questions and wants examples of how big ideas work in practice.

¤ They are more concrete than abstract thinkers, and questioning is their way of understanding and getting through to what things mean.

¤ They will be irritated if they sense you do not understand their world and have not set the presentation in the right register to reflect this.

Characteristics

¤ Like the Visionary, this archetype is comfortable with the big picture, but they use dialogue as a way of understanding new ideas. They enjoy the process of listening, observing and then asking penetrating questions.

¤ To arrive at a full understanding of what they are being told, they will seek out supporting facts, explore alternatives and different angles. They like to weigh up the views of different experts before arriving at their final decision.

¤ They enjoy questioning as a way of progressing ideas but do not necessarily expect the perfect answer/solution to each question. But they will become irritated if the presenter cannot handle this dialectic approach to developing ideas.

How to interact

¤ Don't be too theoretical.

¤ Translate abstract ideas into concrete business applications.

¤ Have worked examples of every conceptual point you are presenting.

¤ Anticipate what are the reasonable questions to which you must know the answer.

¤ Be confident in your handling of questions - this archetype will smell any desperation!

- Be comfortable with the question and answer format for developing ideas, and do not become nervous or anxious when faced with a penetrating question.

Archetype 4: The Worrier - they can see some opportunities but tend to focus on risks which makes them reluctant to take action

Overview

- This archetype tends to be risk averse and suffers from free-floating anxiety about taking action (even when there is a well-defined opportunity and a very good chance of success).
- They tend to see life as a *burden* not an *opportunity*.
- The bottle is often seen as half empty rather than half full.

Characteristics

- Worriers struggle to accept that, in business, there may not always be a totally risk free, black and white solution. This archetype does not enjoy dealing with shades of grey. They tend to keep looping through all of the eventualities in the hope this will alleviate their concerns about any risk. But in fact, this tends to exacerbate their concern.
- Talking through a *problem* with this archetype can create even more worry and pressure because it takes them into anxiety inducing complexities. So, care needs to be taken in providing too much *cognitive overload*.
- They tend to not take a decision, but instead procrastinate, delay and put off seizing what could be a good opportunity.

How to interact

- Empathise with their view of the world - be genuine and authentic in your support.
- Work hard to get them to the point of saying *Yes, that makes sense*. Get them to relax - in this way they will be more likely to listen to your solutions to some of their worries.

¤ Don't *talk over them,* as they will leave the conversation at the earliest opportunity. Nor should you talk *at them,* which could be perceived as threatening.

¤ Sensitively and supportively frame the decision choices open to them and outline the pros and cons of the alternatives.

¤ Paint a picture of the consequences of not taking appropriate action. One approach would be to use the *Parallel Universe* storytelling technique. This allows you illustrate what happens if you do X versus what happens if you do Y. Do this in a reassuring and supportive way.

¤ Provide case histories - stories - where similar decisions have led to successful outcomes.

Archetype 5: The Micro Manager - wants to know how an idea would impact on their own, immediate, here and now, local situation

Overview

¤ Micromanagers see the world, and likely success of any project, through the lens of how it will immediately solve problems in their own micro world.

¤ They have difficulty seeing how powerful, visionary, compelling ideas can apply to them. If the presenter cannot explain how a big idea translates into solving their immediate micro problem they will switch off. They need to see how ideas will work in their own region, office or work environment.

¤ In a presentation setting, this archetype stance can lower the energy of others in the room. And if pursued overzealously, this style can destroy confidence in what are compelling visionary ideas. On the upside this perspective gives this archetype a very detailed orientation and helps us test to destruction the viability of new ideas.

Characteristics

¤ They tend to operate more in *System 2* rational, rather than *System 1* emotional, mode when it comes to evaluating arguments and making decisions.

- They see their micromanagement focus as being a positive contribution to the group/presentation rather than as hindering progress and undermining confidence.
- They may struggle to grasp general practical examples of a big idea and demand ever more micro examples that relate to their own world in a way that may not be possible to deliver.

How to interact

- It is important not to be irritated by micro managers who can be oblivious to the effect they are having on other people with their relentless overdetailed focus on their local situation.
- Always acknowledge the importance of providing practical examples to illustrate a bigger point.
- Do the best you can to relate to these individuals' own immediate worlds. But having done this, be assertive in pointing out that, because certain answers cannot be delivered at the micro level, this does *not* mean that the bigger idea does not have merit.
- Reassure this archetype on your ability to access the detail. Explain that even the most professional of presenters are unlikely to have to hand the detail needed to answer every question but explain this can be made available.
- Try to identify detailed, potentially problematic, issues *before* they are raised by micro managers. This will reassure them that you are practical and have an eye for detail. If you are able to also provide some concrete solutions this will help ensure detailed issues do not escalate.
- Encourage the micro manager to see value in understanding the bigger business picture - how others see the issue.

Archetype 6: The Networker - a people person who likes to make sure that everyone is aligned

Overview

- Networkers play an important role in oiling the wheels of the success of projects because they are good with people. They like harmony and alignment. Clearly, this is helpful, but it can represent a rather naive view of the world.

¤ They see projects - the risks and opportunities - through the lens of making sure that a solution does not create any friction or unpleasantness to anyone involved with the venture.

¤ They do not like conflict, and this can get in the way of arriving at the best solution for a particular business problem.

Characteristics

¤ Networkers can give too much weight to the people dimension and the need to create a good atmosphere around any business solution.

¤ They have a need for personal approval and can shy away from conflict. They find it difficult to accept that in certain business situations, conflict and tension comes with the territory of arriving at the best business outcome.

¤ They may also lack the tenacity and persistence to drive through a solution to a problem. They may be outside their comfort zone when asked to engage in some of the harsh political realities and practical detail of actually making things happen.

How to interact

¤ Networkers like to see themselves as being successful and a valued part of the team. So, complimenting them on the role they are playing will help you get their support.

¤ Acknowledging their role as a people expert, a specialist in networking and the sharing of ideas, will keep them motivated. They can help you get buy-in to the outcome you want to achieve.

¤ Make it easy for them to understand the complexities and details that are often critical to success.

¤ Be supportive when they are forced beyond their comfort zone into taking business action.

¤ Networkers will often be persuaded more by the emotional arguments, rather than more rational detailed statistical explanations. So, factor this into the way you deal with them.

¤ Do not put them on the spot by asking them to create a concrete output against a tight deadline - this could spook them!

FREQUENTLY ASKED QUESTIONS

Question One: Is it always possible to construct a communication that covers what you feel the audience must know, but at the same time is not too complicated for specific audience archetypes to absorb?

Answer: It is a judgement call. But, as a general rule *less is more.* You need to experiment in finding a solution that finds the *sweet spot* between doing justice to critical complexity and not oversimplifying the issue.

Question Two: What advice do you have about delivering detailed technical information?

Answer: It is helpful to think of a presentation as containing *hot zones,* where there will be a fast presentation of big ideas and concepts delivered at speed. Here the presenter will keep the presentation at a high level. The aim is to energise the audience and encourage them to think inspirational thoughts.

But there will also be some *cool zones,* where you slow down the presentation and focus closely on the detail. Given this, it can be helpful to explain in advance when you are about to enter a cool zone and will be presenting material that is going to require concentration.

Question Three: How do you deal with an audience that is split into two groups? Some feel more comfortable with hard numbers and struggle to find merit in softer, qualitative evidence. But others may have *figure phobia* and only feel at ease with qualitative evidence.

Answer: We would recommend a Holistic approach to presenting data as a way of appealing to *both* the qualitative and quantitative mindsets. Apply the concept of evidence having *Weight, Power* and *Direction.*

Top Tip

In handling challenging archetypes *massage the egos* before you deliver your message. Do not assume all audience members will be instantly receptive to the elegance and power of your message. Assume that you *first* need to manage the egos and personalities in play. This often can be just as important as crafting the message itself.

 Best Next Move

On your next project, review the profile of your audience. Identify those stakeholders who could block the progress of your insight or stand in the way of turning your insights into action. For each stakeholder identify the specific communications strategies and techniques you will adopt to ensure you fully engage with them - and drive home your message.

SUMMARY

We have identified six different *Stakeholder Archetypes* with which it is important to familiarise yourself so you can overcome any blocks that may stand in the way of them receiving your message.

Archetype 1: The Visionary - wants the big picture helicopter view. Make sure that you provide a high level strategic account of the solution to the business question (tactical details can be addressed elsewhere).

Archetype 2: The Dominant Personality - suspicious of an expert's facts and believe their own instinctive intuitive point of view must be right. Do not take an overly aggressive stance - soak up their argument, listen and relate to their point of view, then gradually build trust to progress to being more assertive.

Archetype 3: The Questioner - seeks to understand by questioning and needs examples of ideas in practice. Do not be too theoretical, make sure you always have practical examples to reinforce every point you are making.

Archetype 4: The Worrier - they can see some opportunities but tend to focus on risks which makes them reluctant to take action. Empathise with their view of the world, be authentic with your support and be reassuring.

Archetype 5: The Micro Manager - wants to know how an idea would impact on their own, immediate, here and now local situation. Acknowledge the importance of practical examples, provide illustrations, relate to their world where you can but do not let this relentless line of micro questioning undermine your presentation.

Archetype 6: The Networker - a people person who likes to make sure that everyone is aligned. Acknowledge their role as a people-experts, but make sure you engage them with the business realities of some of their thinking.

Next, we look at *Managing Resistance* - dealing with any barriers that are standing in the way of turning your insight into action.

18 MANAGING RESISTANCE
How to handle any resistance to, or poor interpretation of, insight messages

A key part of turning insights into action is the skill of handling any stakeholder resistance to, or a flawed interpretation of, insight messages designed to bring about change.

GUIDING PRINCIPLES

Principle One: Be aware of cognitive biases that may affect the way stakeholders receive insight messages

It is important to be aware of the different ways in which people think and react when they are presented with problems or information: the biases that can affect them arriving at an informed interpretation of the insight evidence.

Principle Two: Ensure you have a strategy for handling any resistance to your message

Develop your own personal style to ensure you bring the appropriate level of objectivity and emotional control to scenarios where there is stakeholder resistance to your ideas.

Principle Three: Develop strategies for dealing with ill-informed decision-making

Be aware of different techniques for handling sub-optimum or dysfunctional decision-making that will require an intervention to realign the decision with the evidence.

KEY ACTIONS

Action 1: Know what biases and dysfunctionality block information being correctly processed

A start point for coping with behaviours that could block the successful activation of an insight is to be aware of - and take avoiding action on - common resistances to even the most compelling of insights being accepted.

Let's look at some of the factors that may stand in the way of your insight message being received.

Denial that the challenge exists

There is often a fundamental lack of awareness that a challenge or problem even exists. Audiences often only see things as they want to see them, not necessarily as they really are. There is a tendency for some people to switch off and be blind to certain issues. Thus, the start-point for guiding the audience through your evidence is to ensure they are *seeing it as it is*.

A failure to accept the facts

There will be scenarios where stakeholders hold deeply entrenched positions based on long established beliefs. These create a prejudice against, and reluctance to accept, new incoming evidence. Knute Rockne said, *'People don't so much have a point of view, they just rearrange their prejudices!'* Be prepared to challenge entrenched positions.

Lazy, default and stereotypical thinking

Remove any muddle or confusion around the core problem. Much flawed decision-making stems from the fact that stakeholders have defaulted to working on the symptoms not the root cause of the problem. Challenge received wisdom and call out the big underlying, but flawed, assumptions that could be hijacking sound evidence-based decision-making.

The false belief that action has already been taken to address this issue

People can come to believe that a problem has been solved simply because it has been identified. This is referred to as *norming*. The classic illustration of this was the Challenger space shuttle disaster. It was known that there could be a potential problem with a seal (O-ring) in the rocket engine at low temperature launching conditions.

This problem - risk - became accepted (seen as normal) on the grounds that such low temperatures were very unlikely to occur. This was flawed thinking. The problem should have been fixed earlier. There were low temperatures on the day of the launch. The resulting explosion was an accident waiting to happen.

Reluctance to accept the evidence because it is too disruptive

Another barrier to informed decision-making is the rejection of new evidence that could create disruptive organisational outcomes and/or personal hassle for the stakeholders. The audience comes to resent change even though it is ultimately for the good. You need to be motivational in encouraging stakeholders to embrace change.

Emotional investment

When people have sunk a lot of emotional investment in a particular venture, they find it difficult to abandon the project, even when all the evidence points in this direction.

The reluctance to make a U-turn and change a point of view

People are often reluctant to do a U-turn because they think this could be seen as a sign of weakness.

Lightening will not strike twice

There is a mistaken belief that, because a problem has occurred several times, it will not happen again. This is called the *Gambler's Fallacy:* believing that future probabilities are altered by past events where in fact they remain unchanged.

Hasty knee-jerk reactions

In today's time pressured, stress-filled environment some decision-makers do not take the time and space needed for clear deep thinking. Decisions are taken without enough elapsed time to reflect on what is actually happening. It is important to have strategies in place to steer the audience away from superficial knee-jerk reactions

Too great a reliance on intuition

Individuals can default to too much intuitive, emotion-based decision-making. They do not arrive at the decision-making sweet spot: the right balance between System 1 and System 2 thinking - *informed intuition.*

Group decision-making

Poor decisions may occur when stakeholders are overly influenced by what the wider stakeholder group thinks.

Priming effects

If an idea is framed or introduced in a particular way, this priming will affect the likelihood of a particular decision being made.

Selective favouring of accessible evidence

Some people have a tendency to act on top of mind, readily available and easy to obtain data, rather than looking more thoroughly at the full comprehensive range of evidence.

Over influenced by the easiest to understand evidence

Here the thinking is that something must be true because it is simple to understand, thus rejecting complex but more useful information.

Overly simplistic rules of thumb

Decision-makers may have a simple intuitive heuristic they apply to understand their world. In some cases, these may be helpful, but in others they may no longer be relevant.

Flawed causality

There is a belief that A is driven by B when in fact this is not true.

Favour gains to losses

People think differently when an issue is couched in terms of the *losses* associated with a particular decision, as opposed to being framed around the *gains* that could be achieved with this approach.

Flawed self-perception

Some people deceive themselves about their capability to resolve challenges - we may not be as good as we think we are!

Poor assessment of others' reaction

Some people have an exaggerated sense of the power and influence they can exert over events once the decision is made.

Arbitrary decision-making benchmarks

It is quite common for people to say *let's go for a 50/50 solution* when there may be no logic to this particular split.

Action 2: Develop your own personal strategy for staying in control

The start point for dealing with resistance is to have total clarity around your purpose - what you want to achieve. Ensure you are acting with integrity and intentionality to achieve a mutually acceptable goal. Demonstrate authenticity and genuineness. Act in the interest of the overall good - do not be driven by self-interest.

The effective management of difficult situations starts with having self-awareness and self-control. This provides the platform for ensuring disruptive behaviours do not throw you off course. Make sure you have control over how you will *initially* react to different situations. Let's look at some models and techniques for achieving this.

The Choice Moment model

When confronted with a challenge it is important to create time and space between the stimulus (*cause*) and your reaction (the *effect*). Thus, if an audience member makes an *intervention* (the stimulus/cause) to which you react immediately, or in an over-emotional way, this could have a negative counter-productive *effect*.

To address this, we suggest you create a *Choice Moment* - a time out period - in which you avoid overreaction and decide on your best next move. Let us break down the sequence of events in a typical scenario:

¤ There is the initial *cause* (stimulus)

- This could prompt you to *react* in a hasty emotional way leading to an unhelpful outcome.
- You have a split second to *reflect* on these negative consequences and *review* the full range of options open to you.
- Then there is a choice moment where you need to decide on what is the best *reaction* to this *cause* - the one with the best outcome.
- This would then lead to the *outcome* (effect) of your reaction.

The choice moment model will help you deal with challenging stakeholder alignment issues and guide your intervention strategy. It will help you to avoid over reacting to what you may perceive to be a negative or unhelpful intervention.

Use this choice moment pause to reflect on the options open to you, and the likely outcomes, before you respond or take action. Pick a response that will get you into the right space: do <u>not</u> go for an option that will create a negative reaction from the other person.

I'm OK/You're OK

It can be helpful to work through various scenarios to arrive at a *I'm OK/You're OK* solution in aligning with stakeholders. It is often easy to find a temporary win through an *I'm OK,* but your audience member is *Not OK,* position. Similarly, it is easy to give in to a situation where you are *Not OK,* but your audience member *Is OK.*

Your goal should be to arrive at the *I'm OK/You're OK* sweet spot - demonstrating sensitivity and empathy with the other individual's position, but still ensuring you achieve your purpose.

Be the sponge - apply the softly/softly approach

Never take things personally. Bring your own ego under control: recognise that your job is to help the audience make sound decisions. Be willing to *soak up* some of the ego issues in the room in the interest of getting over your message. Sometimes you will have to let issues go to achieve the ultimate outcome.

You need to decide which battles to fight - where it is legitimate for you to challenge and make an intervention, and where this falls outside your remit.

Be aware of where there is a mission critical issue with massive consequences that you *must* address. Distinguish this from an irritating issue that you should really let go. You need to know where you can fight and win a battle and where it may be better to retreat.

Action 3: Cultivate a conflict management style that works for you

There is no one right conflict management approach. But, in managing conflict, it is helpful to have a mental model for understanding yourself and others. One model you may find helpful shows an individual's concern for *achieving personal goals* on one axis, and on the other axis, their *concern for relationships*. In the diagram below, we identify five different management styles.

A conflict management framework

The Shark: The focus is on achieving personal goals but at the cost of relationships.

The Teddy Bear: The focus is primarily around relationships rather than achieving personal goals.

The Turtle: There is no focus on either achieving personal goals nor on having concern for relationships.

The Owl: The focus is on collaboration to achieve both personal goals and create effective relationships.

The Fox: This is about achieving an appropriate compromise between personal goals and relationships.

This framework will help you know where *you* sit and help you build an understanding of different stakeholder perspectives on an issue. The framework is not designed to provide specific prescriptions on exactly what to do in different scenarios.

However, it is probably not a good idea to play the role of the *shark*, where you constantly go on the attack! Neither is it likely to be productive to be the *turtle* who goes into its shell and avoids dealing with issues. And, being a *teddy bear* is also rather limiting.

Being an *owl* is an option. And, for insight professionals, being *flexible, but assertive* on critical issues - like the *fox*- is often a good way forward.

Using this framework will provide a focus for rehearsing the way different styles might work with various stakeholders. You need to be spontaneous and intuitive on the day. But putting in the hard yards in advance in knowing what language and techniques are likely to work best with stakeholder archetypes, from different parts of the *conflict matrix*, will improve your chances of overcoming resistance to your insight message.

Action 4: Cultivate your negotiation skills - know how to secure a Yes

Cultivate the art of knowing how to secure a mutually acceptable *Yes*. Below we provide some tips on negotiating successful outcomes.

Focus on the key goals and principles, not on the personalities

Move the discussion away from personalities towards focusing on the fundamental goals of the negotiation. Do not classify participants as being a *friend* or an *adversary*. Think of participants as *problem solvers*. Do not position the negotiation task as being about *victory* or *loss*. Instead position this as both parties working towards a *mutually beneficial goal*.

Take care with the language used to describe the position of different players

Shift the agenda away from identifying players as making *demands* or as individuals needing to make *concessions*. Move the language away from people who you *trust* or *distrust* on a particular position. Also avoid setting up the discussion around *hard* and *soft* positions. Instead, move the agenda towards there being *trust in all parties* and there being a common interest in staying focused on solving the common problem.

Do not focus on red line positions - seek common interests

Move away from the idea of people making *threats* in the form of arguing for a non-negotiable *red line* position. Instead work with the idea of exploring interests in a way that avoids the concept of red lines.

Develop options for mutual gain

Do not get locked into the idea of there being only *one single answer* that everyone must accept but move towards the notion of there being *multiple options* for consideration.

Focus on using objective criteria

Do not position the negotiation as being a *contest of wills* where it is about applying personal pressure to reach a result. Frame the negotiation around stakeholders being prepared to listen to compelling fundamental principles, rather than having to yield to undue pressure.

Develop the Third Corner perspective

Look at issues from the *outside-in - third corner -* perspective. This will encourage you to identify the key concepts in play and minimise the chances of you getting involved in personality conflicts. This will help to depersonalise differing points of view by identifying the main principle or concept at the core of what is being discussed.

For example, to take the heat out of a passionate discussion about the merits or otherwise of *private* education, focus on the two (arguably) *equally important* principles in play here: one's *right to choose how to spend one's money* and *equal opportunity* in education.

Managing the decision script

If the decision process and outcome is described by different stakeholders in various ways, with each adding their *spin* on events, this does not make for cohesive alignment. You do not want different stakeholders sending out varying messages and signals about the process by which the decision was made and its final resolution.

To offset the chances of this happening, and to keep everyone *on-message*, ensure there is a *script* that all parties are working from when they describe exactly how they arrived at the decision.

If all stakeholders share a similar account of exactly how the decision process was accomplished, this enhances the chances of the outcome being successfully actioned. This scripting will help get buy-in from stakeholders to the decision.

Action 5: Intervene if you feel the wrong decision, or a flawed interpretation of the evidence, is being made

It is not necessarily your responsibility to make the final decision. However, if you feel the consequences of a decision could be disastrous for the organisation, then integrity dictates that you should intervene.

Below we review some scenarios where dysfunctional behaviour and cognitive biases may be adversely affecting the quality of the decision. For each we outline the avoidance action you might consider.

A decision based on familiar business heuristics that are no longer relevant

There are situations where decision-makers place undue weight on previously successful heuristics (rules of thumb) that have usually led them to the right decision. They apply these to situations where these criteria are no longer relevant. In so doing they arrive at the wrong decision. The action to take here is to:

Change the angle of vision: This could be as simple as coaxing the stakeholder to articulate these previous experiences with the aim of drawing out the fact that the former heuristic is no longer relevant.

217

A decision based on an overly optimistic forecast of market potential or an underestimation of the effectiveness of likely competitive response

There can be a tendency for certain decision-makers to be excessively optimistic about the future, and their ability to influence it. This can lead to a culture of over-confidence and over-optimism that makes for poor decision-making. One option is to:

Encourage recognition of the uncertainty associated with a particular decision: Use tools, such as *Scenario Planning,* to spell out - using accepted metrics - what is likely to actually happen in practice. This will help temper this over-optimism.

Poor decisions based on stability bias - decision-makers being reluctant to depart from the status quo

Decision-makers often tend to anchor around what is happening now and cannot see the need for change. This is about having an inbuilt bias towards holding onto business activities that should be dropped. It is often helpful to:

Jolt people out of business as usual thinking: Apply some melodrama! *Shake things up* by mapping out the likely business outcome and financial results of slavishly following a business as usual approach. Compare and contrast a conventional approach with a more radical and different way of doing things.

Personal interests are leading to poor decision-making

It is natural enough that, within any one organisation, that there maybe be conflict between individuals and teams based on *turf wars* and competing career aspirations. Thus, there could be situations where individuals might work against the optimum corporate decision in order to defend their own interests. Here, focus on:

Making these biases explicit: Create transparency to pinpoint what is the most beneficial - optimum - corporate solution. This will help to draw out into the open any biases in play and make it difficult for certain individuals to change/influence the debate towards their own preferred action.

Poor decision-making resulting from deep rooted (dominant) personality conflicts

A strong warning sign that things may be going off course is when there is an *absence of dissent* within the organisation. This results from a dominant personality who thrives because others acquiesce - they are frightened to speak up. It creates an unhealthy culture. Everyone in the room knows this dominant personality is unlikely to change their mind and so they slavishly fall in line with the leader's prescribed *solution*. To address a dominant personality challenge:

> **Depersonalise the debate by encouraging other views:** Highlight the value of putting diversity and different points of view into the decision-making process.

A critical decision is not made - procrastination sets in and the insight sits on the shelf

Address the *procrastination syndrome:* situations where a delay in making a decision is justified on the grounds that extra time will somehow improve the quality of the decision. On occasion this can be true but, in many cases, it is simply a way of putting off making a decision. One approach is to:

> **Map out the consequences of delay:** Make it crystal clear that there are no benefits to delaying the decision. Alert stakeholders to the dangers of making a decision too late in the process to influence the desired outcome. Drive home the point that, as a general rule, fast decision-making is good decision-making.

Decisions being hijacked by individuals who have deeply held beliefs that are not necessarily supported by the hard facts

Poor decision-making often stems from being overly influenced by emotion - too much weight is given to intuition. What we are trying to achieve is *informed intuition* - where the judgement of key stakeholders is compatible with the evidence. A way forward here is to:

> **Address critical beliefs:** Encourage individuals to move to a position where their beliefs and the evidence are more aligned. Focus on unpacking the critical belief or assumption that lies at the heart of the assertion or claim

being made. Explore with the stakeholder, in a sensitive way, why they hold this particular belief: how they have come to believe this to be *true*.

Decision-makers do not appreciate other stakeholder perspectives

Poor decision-making often stems from a blinkered view about how other people feel about the issue. It can be helpful to employ:

The Delphi technique: This is a process whereby a team of decision-makers offer an initial opinion. This is then shared in an open and transparent way with other decision-making team members. This gives everyone the opportunity to revise their initial view in light of feedback from others. We are not suggesting that the full Delphi methodology is always employed. But the notion of sharing and allowing people to see whether their own initial view is an *outlier* one, or more in line with other team members, can be helpful.

A failure to understand the consequences of taking different decisions

Sometimes, resistance to accepting a message stems from a failure to fully understand the consequences of taking a particular course of action. It pays dividends to:

Outline the future: The insight professional could play a decision facilitation role in applying storytelling techniques to drive home the consequences of taking particular lines of action. In the *Insight Story Builder*, we outlined a number of Story Tool techniques - including the *Parallel Universe* and/or *Time Machine* - to map out consequences.

Perfectionism syndrome - an enemy that stands in the way of insight being actioned

Some decision-makers will not make a decision until they have all the *perfect* information needed to make the right decision. In some cases, the decision to obtain more information is a wise one. But often extra information will *not* improve the quality of the decision. Highlight this principle:

Diminishing returns: As a general rule, there are diminishing returns from investing time and energy in teasing out the last drops of difficult to access information on a topic. Rarely does this extra time and effort substantially improve the quality of the final decision. The quest for *perfect* information can become an excuse for not taking action.

Action 6: Anticipate, and be prepared to handle, audience resistance on the day of the presentation

To complete your toolkit of strategies and tactics for handling resistance to your insight message, be ready with techniques to handle different stakeholder questions *on the day*. It is helpful to have pre-prepared responses that you can use to deal with any attempts to undermine the points you are making.

Work hard to anticipate the likely reaction of different stakeholders. Create your own luck by being prepared to respond to audience interventions. Louis Pasteur said, '*Chance favours only the prepared mind*'. Below we provide some interventions that stakeholders may make that could undermine your position, together with suggestions of ways in which these could be addressed.

I don't believe it!

Some stakeholders become insistent that certain facts cannot possibly be true. They give their feelings and emotions too high a weight, in relation to the hard facts. This can lead to a rejection of a powerful insight-driven recommendation. A helpful response here is to find ways of contextualising this questionable received wisdom in a way that drives home the implications of taking this highly personal, but outlier, position. This could be:

> *We understand why you have this particular view based on your experience, but let's look at your viewpoint in the context of a range of other expert opinions.*

That advice is too general - I want something more specific

Stakeholders may undermine the authority of your insight-based recommendation by arguing that your advice is *too general*. They believe that you cannot provide *legitimate* advice unless you can match their sector-specific knowledge. This *my business is completely different* mantra is rarely true and needs challenging. Here, a useful approach is to be forthright:

> *We respect your own specific sector knowledge, but experience across a range of sectors tells us there are certain fundamental truths that apply across all sectors - including yours. It would be risky to ignore these general principles.*

Death by a thousand cuts

A series of small pedantic interventions made throughout your presentation may cumulatively begin to undercut your central argument. These comments begin to create doubt about the wisdom and authority of your core point. You need to be assertive - an effective response might be:

> *I would like to say that, even after factoring the important detailed points you make about the analysis, this does not affect my fundamental belief that the overall evidence is still telling us that we should do X not Y.*

This was never raised in the focus group I attended!

You need to be prepared for a situation where a fundamental point you are raising was *not* one that was observed *directly* by a stakeholder. A response here could be:

> *We can assure you, having analysed the X hours of transcripts from Y respondents, attending Z focus groups, that the fundamental driving attitude in play is A. This was the view overwhelmingly cited by the majority of participants in the research. It is sometimes the case that there will be an outlier focus group where a particular point is not made.*

The not invented here syndrome

Some stakeholders resist excellent ideas simply because they were not *directly* involved in the origination process. Here it comes down to being explicit in your response:

> *We have taken into account that this idea came from outside the team immediately responsible for running this project. But all the evidence tells us that this is a robust, valid compelling idea, and the consequences of rejecting this idea would constitute a major missed opportunity.*

This idea was successful before/elsewhere

Sometimes it is argued that an idea that failed in a particular region will still work because *elsewhere in the world* this idea had been a tremendous success.

This narrative implies there must have been something wrong with the research process - otherwise surely the idea would have worked in this particular local region. Again, an assertive response is called for:

We have taken into account the successful track record of X elsewhere in the world. But we must stress that a series of critically important and highly specific cultural factors dramatically change customer acceptance of this idea in this particular region.

FREQUENTLY ASKED QUESTIONS

Question One: How do you handle audience members who attack you as a person, rather than the arguments you are presenting?

Answer: Make sure you take a *Choice Moment:* do not act in an emotional way that you will then regret. Another technique to depersonalise an issue is to step back and look in from the *third corner* - take the ternary conceptual position. Identify the key concepts and principles in play and focus on these. This can help turn the attention away from the personalities.

Question Two: What if there are deep-seated political agendas that cannot be resolved at the time of the presentation - how do you handle these situations?

Answer: It could be beneficial to initiate a short *cooling-off* period for people to reflect on the different views being expressed - returning later to see whether there is a mutually acceptable next step. There is also merit in agreeing to return to a contentious issue after critical *relevant* missing information has been obtained.

Question Three: How do you decide when to *let issues go* rather than upset or alienate an audience member?

Answer: It is a difficult balancing act. If the issue in contention is not *mission critical,* then there may be merit in letting the issue go and allowing the audience member to save face. However, if the point is critical to you getting over your core message then you will have to persevere with strategies to hit home your point.

Top Tip

Master the *Choice Moment* technique: approach any resistance to your message, and/or misinterpretation of what you are trying to say, with a calm, in control perspective.

Best Next Move

On your next project, identify the key resistances to, or misinterpretations of, the evidence that you could face from different stakeholders. Take time out to reflect on what strategies and styles will work best for you - which *levers to pull* - to deal with these tricky situations.

SUMMARY

Managing resistance to, or the poor interpretation of, insight messages starts with being aware of the different cognitive biases that can stand in the way of stakeholders receiving messages in an appropriate way.

Cultivate a mindset that allows you to stay in full emotional control when dealing with deep-seated tensions that can surface with, or between, stakeholders.

Success lies in putting in the time to develop a conflict resolution style that will work for you.

Develop the art of getting to a *Yes* through skilful negotiation.

Insight professionals also need to be able to develop strategies that will address flawed or suboptimum decision-making.

Be prepared to handle questions and issues that can arise on the day and could create further resistance to your message being accepted.

Next, we look at *Implementation Strategies* - techniques to help ensure insight-based solutions are activated.

19 IMPLEMENTATION
How to support the activation of insight-driven decisions

One of the biggest frustrations for customer insight professionals is to find that, after all their hard work, no action is taken on their insight. So, we now focus on strategies to help customer insight professionals work with stakeholders to *implement* insights.

GUIDING PRINCIPLES

Principle One: Follow a systematic activation process

Effective implementation benefits from putting in place a systematic process, rather than just hoping that some kind of action will be taken after an insight presentation.

Principle Two: Ensure there is a high energy Project Champion

It is important to have someone in the insight team who will ensure that action is taken. This requires high energy and a willingness to take personal responsibility for bridging the evidence/action gap.

Principle Three: Take personal responsibility for identifying and overcoming barriers

Carefully review the techniques available to you to overcome any possible resistance to the implementation of an insight. Make it your job to resolve these - take action and do not leave this to others.

KEY ACTIONS

Action 1: Follow a step-by-step implementation process

Implementation benefits from following a disciplined and systematic process. In order to bridge the gap between the identification of an insight and its implementation, there needs to be some form of implementation process - usually a series of follow-up workshops.

It is difficult to transition from an insight presentation into the implementation of this insight without some activation process being in place.

Different organisations will have different implementation approaches. But at a high level, these approaches tend to have the following distinct phases.

The review, alignment and prioritisation phase

The process begins with a review of what has been learnt from the insight presentation. Here, ensure your insight message has got through. If there are any doubts about this, be proactive and take responsibility for finding ways of reinforcing the insight on which you want stakeholders to take action.

One option is to change the original communications medium and/or sharpen the earlier message. For example, you could send a short video of the main presentation highlights or send out a quiz style question to trigger engagement, such as *Do you know how many of your customers buy from you only once and never return?*

Once there has been engagement and comprehension of the insight message, then prioritise the key actions required. Then make sure there is alignment with stakeholders about next steps. One option for achieving this is as follows:

Review the customer journey

One technique to get the implementation phase underway is to plot the pre-purchase, purchase and post-purchase customer journey for the product or service in question.

Specifically, there would be a clarification of the goals of each part of the customer journey and a description of exactly what should happen at each point in the journey, followed by a summary of the different experiences typically faced by customers.

This leads to a review of the emotional *highs* and *lows* in the customer experience. This process then culminates by prioritising the big ticket *emotional customer needs* and *pain points* that need to be addressed.

The involvement, embellishment and enrichment phase

The next part of the implementation process invites stakeholders to be more closely involved with the insight findings. Here there could be *co-creativity* sessions, where the insight professionals and stakeholders work together to enrich, embellish and flesh out a particular insight.

The goal is to pinpoint how an insight can best be converted into a value proposition, and then into a new product or innovation. The following is an illustration of a technique that can be applied to secure involvement with stakeholders.

The borrow and adapt technique

This involves assembling different mini case studies of best practice from competitors related to the product and service idea you are aspiring to deliver. Do this by setting up a gallery of these mini case studies that participants can study.

Individuals could then borrow ideas from the gallery and work out how to adapt and improve them to address the customer emotional needs and pain points identified at the review phase.

This approach could then be supplemented with techniques, such as *60 Ideas in a Minute*. Based on their analysis of the customer journey and review of the gallery, participants are asked to come up with up to 60 different ways of addressing the emotional needs and pain points they have identified.

The testing, experimentation and trial phase

The next part of the typical implementation process involves building on the enrichment phase to develop different value propositions. One technique is:

The value proposition acid test

The aim is to identify a world-class customer experience: the optimum value proposition - a product/service solution. This process is an interrogation of the putative value proposition. It asks the following questions: *Is it unique?* (and if so, *What is the evidence for this?*) *Does it have the wow factor? Is it critically important to customers' lives? Is it credible? Is it easily understood? Is it easily communicated? Can you build the operating capability to deliver the promise?*

Action 2: Successful implementation requires a Project Champion

It is important that there is an individual within the customer insight team who is confident and capable in playing the *project champion* role in driving through insight. This project champion role is critical: they need to operate with presence, focus and intentionality to drive the implementation of insight. They need to have high levels of energy and tenacity. They always bring their *A-Game* to the table.

The successful Project Champion will be an Energy Radiator and Problem Simplifier

An effective project champion will have the following fundamental characteristics.

Energy Radiator

Everything they do will radiate enthusiasm and high energy. They will bring intentionality and purpose to the task of driving through insights. They will not be an *energy drain*: someone who saps the enthusiasm from everyone around them and has a negative rather than a positive *can-do* attitude.

Problem Simplifier

They will be able to find the most elegant solution to any problem. To cite Einstein, they know how to, *make things simple but not simpler*. They will not be a *problem confuser* who does not know the difference between *important complexity* that needs resolving, and *unnecessary confusion* that should be eliminated.

Team working

Critically the project champion will also need to be comfortable working constructively with other insight team members, each of whom will play supporting and complementary roles. Typically, this will involve the project champion knowing how to successfully work with the following team member *archetypes*:

The King: The figurehead who is leading the insight function within the organisation.

The Magician: The creative team member who is crafting innovative solutions and developing value propositions.

The Warrior: The individual who is good at getting tasks completed on time.

The Networker: The team member who leads the way in facilitating interaction between the insight team and other stakeholders involved in the process.

Action 3: Know how to minimise fixed and encourage growth mindset thinking

We have introduced the idea of there being a *growth mindset* and a *fixed mindset*. You need to manage stakeholders who fall into these two broad categories.

The growth mindset

This mindset is characterised by being receptive to innovation, change and the implementation of insight-driven ideas. Those with a growth mindset have a desire to learn with a tendency to embrace challenges and persist in the face of setbacks. They see effort as a path to mastery, learn from criticism and find lessons and inspiration in the success of others.

The fixed mindset

Fixed mindset personalities tend to avoid challenges, get defensive and give up easily. They often see effort as fruitless or not worthwhile. They also often ignore constructive feedback and feel threatened by the success of others. In sum, this is a deep-seated outlook that makes them resistant to new ideas and is a barrier to the implementation of insight.

Develop strategies to encourage action by fixed mindset stakeholders

One way forward is to work in a constructive way with fixed mindset stakeholders to make them feel more comfortable about change. Specifically, address the fact that a fixed mindset is characterised by having *limiting beliefs* about what is possible.

Limiting beliefs can play themselves out in negativity that becomes a *self-imposed* barrier or boundary. This can trigger a range of *self-sabotaging* behaviours.

Fear of failure

These limiting beliefs may stem from a *fear of failure*. These individuals would rather continue doing what they have always done (and getting the same failed results) rather than running the risk of doing something new that is not totally guaranteed to succeed.

Fear of success!

But limiting beliefs may also be rooted in a *fear of success*. These people prefer to stay in their comfort zone and maintain the status quo rather than respond to a change that could catapult them into the limelight.

The experienced insight consultant will focus on encouraging greater confidence and self-belief amongst stakeholders with a fixed mindset and encourage them on the path to cultivating a more *growth* outlook when executing insight-driven ideas.

Action 4: Select effective technique(s) to overcome barriers to the implementation of insight

There are a number of different consultative techniques to consider in order to unlock barriers to the implementation of insight-driven ideas.

Minimise the risk

One way of unblocking an issue that is standing in the way of implementation is to reduce the risk around this issue. This could be achieved through a simple low-cost experiment that focuses solely on the major stumbling blocks to implementing an idea.

This is based on the principle of first testing a *minimum viable product* version of your idea. This involves focusing on the fundamental success factors before developing the idea any further.

Does this come in a size 7?

An illustration of this thinking was the introduction of the first *online* shoe business. Before the company set up an online infrastructure, they created a simple website just to explore whether people would be prepared to buy shoes online. When they knew the demand was there, they then invested in the full online implementation process.

Connections not alternatives

One technique to help reduce emotional anxieties around the fear of change is to apply the *connections not alternatives* model we referred to earlier.

There is often resistance to an idea that is suddenly presented as a stark alternative to what stakeholders were previously thinking or expecting. Many prefer ideas that connect with what has happened in the past. By focusing on connections not alternatives, the idea is that you will encourage individuals to see the merit of pursuing a new course of action.

Individuals can be tempted to consider a new, even radical, way of thinking about an issue if they can see some connection between the new approach and how things are now or were in the past.

Opportunities and barriers

Outline the *opportunities* of the idea including pinpointing the key drivers that are motivating customers. This will get buy-in to the potential of the insight for building growth and profitability.

Then identify any *barrier*s or *resistance*s that might stand in the way of delivering this opportunity.

Next, look at possible *solutions* to deal with each of these barriers. Here you could engage stakeholders in co-creativity and brainstorming sessions.

Take the first step

This technique is predicated on the fact that stakeholders are more likely to implement a big idea if they can see a small specific first action they can take to get things underway.

This initial progress then builds belief that the initiative is achievable and encourages further action. Think of this as *Where there's a way, there's a will* (reworking the familiar proverb).

How do I look?

A simple example would be weight-loss. Once someone sees they have lost a few pounds in the first week, then this initial progress is likely to encourage them to stay with their diet/fitness programme.

Involve stakeholders early in the insight process

One way of getting insights actioned is to involve stakeholders in the insight creation process. Stakeholders could, for example, be part of creative focus group sessions looking at different value proposition ideas.

We know that, when people have assembled their own IKEA furniture, they become more positive towards IKEA than those who did not - the *IKEA effect*.

Immerse stakeholders in the proposed insight solution

On certain projects it may be possible to involve stakeholders in the recommended insight solution. For example, if there is a particular app, enhancement to the website, or improvement to product packaging, then you could invite stakeholders to immerse themselves in the insight-driven solution or experience.

- You could encourage stakeholders to use *only* the new version of a product for a 24-hour period, rather than the existing product (with the aim of demonstrating its benefits).

- Another idea is to ask stakeholders to take a product with the USP of durability and robustness and ask them to test the product to destruction over a short period.

- One further idea might be to ask stakeholders to be a *mystery shopper* and test out a new improvement, such as the company's updated customer complaints service.

Provide rolling feedback

One further technique to help with the implementation of ideas is to unfold the emerging insight story on a rolling basis. The process of providing initial feedback and following this later with further findings could help the implementation of an insight.

Action 5: Avoid mission drift: closely monitor the implementation process

Small changes - made at the implementation stage - to the specification of a product or service tested in the insight research may radically alter the likely success of the idea. Take action if you feel such changes are misrepresenting the original insight. Explain how such revisions will impact on the initial assessment of the likelihood of success.

Let's double the price

Research was conducted on the introduction of a new magazine in the UK showing a market opportunity and a decision was taken to go ahead. But the green light from the research was predicated on the fact that the magazine would be broadly the same price as its competitors.

But after the insight presentation, a management decision was taken to make the magazine twice the price of its main competitors. There was a mistaken belief that the quality of the magazine would warrant this price hike. But this was not the case. So eventually there had to be some back tracking on pricing.

Action 6: Develop the Action Mindset

The successful insight professional will cultivate an *action mindset* in implementing insight. Below we list the key high performance traits associated with this ability to act and successfully drive the change agenda. The successful insight professional will:

Have a laser-like business focus

They are able to focus on prioritising the critical must-do activities that will *move the needle* and eliminate distractions that stand in the way of delivering these priority goals.

Operate with clarity of purpose and intentionality

They have a crystal clear sense of *purpose* in everything they do. They know exactly what change they want to bring about from an insight and channel all of their efforts and energy into achieving this purpose.

Apply Occam's Razor

This tells us that *all things being equal, the simplest solution is usually the best*. It is about eliminating confusion from the process - whilst addressing critical complexity.

Bring presence and their A-Game to every task

They will *be there*. Successful implementation pivots around insight professionals always turning up with the best possible version of themselves - their A-Game. It is about showing up with self-belief and having presence - exuding the confidence to persuade stakeholders to implement the insight.

Demonstrate entrepreneurial flair and business acumen

They are on top of the business agenda - comfortable operating at the sharp end of business. They are skilled in demonstrating the commercial viability of an insight idea.

Be bold and decisive

They operate with high energy and take personal responsibility for making things happen. They do not procrastinate, and they avoid perfectionism that can delay action.

Act with integrity, courage and commitment

They recognise the fact that they are *admissible evidence* and operate with self-belief and conviction. They have the courage to stand up and defend a sound evidence-based argument. They are totally authentic. They arrive at their position based on a rigorous yet creative analysis of the evidence. They are prepared to speak out against those who intellectually should know better when it comes to the way they have elected to (selectively) *present the facts*.

Show flexible pragmatism

They are at ease with flexible decision-making. They get a line of sight to the general direction of travel, take action, and course correct en route. Today decision-making is often about *building the plane as you fly it*: get the fundamental decision right and then adjust.

Demonstrate the winner's advantage

Self-sabotage is not in their vocabulary. They avoid the loser's curse.

FREQUENTLY ASKED QUESTIONS

Question One: What is the biggest single psychological barrier that explains why many people will not implement a powerful new idea?

> **Answer:** A lot of individuals do not embrace powerful ideas because they are nervous of change - this is linked to a *fear of failure*. They are nervous of opting for something new, for which they may be personally blamed if things go wrong. Given this, the status quo can seem more appealing than opting for change. We have provided various techniques you can use to help reassure stakeholders who may be nervous of change.

Question Two: What skills are most needed by the project champion?

> **Answer:** There are three key traits:
>
> *High energy:* They work at building the energy, tenacity and persistence to follow an initiative through and drive action. People do not *have* high energy - they learn how to *generate* energy. They learn how to boost energy levels so that they can constantly take multiple action.
>
> *Empathy:* They keep their ego under control and work collaboratively with others to achieve the desired outcome.
>
> *Influence and engagement:* They recognise that their role is to *connect, uplift* and demonstrate *presence*: build a positive and constructive dialogue with stakeholders.

Question Three: What is the key to being on top of *Mission Drift*?

> **Answer:** Vigilance - be alert to anything that might undercut how you envisaged your insight working in practice. Identify any changes in the proposed product or service offer that are so dramatically different from what was researched that this change could substantially alter the likely success of the venture. If you sense there has been such a change, you must take action to avoid any negative consequences: do not just assume this will correct itself.

Top Tip

Make sure there is a project champion who can make things happen. They need to be an *energy radiator* and *problem solver*: someone who can work with other team members in driving insights through in a tenacious way.

 Best Next Move

On your next project, create a detailed *playbook* of precisely how you will run your implementation workshop. Identify the implementation process and techniques that you feel are most appropriate to deal with your biggest stakeholder challenges.

SUMMARY

The implementation of insight benefits from having in place a systematic process that can be played out with stakeholders in order to encourage buy-in to key insights.

The implementation of insight also requires an inspirational *Project Champion*.

There is massive benefit to be gained in encouraging stakeholders to adopt the *growth*, not *fixed*, mindset. This is about finding ways to help stakeholders overcome limiting beliefs about what is possible.

Be comfortable with the various techniques for helping overcome barriers to the implementation of insight. These include techniques such as: *Minimise the risk; Connections not alternatives; Opportunities and barriers; Take the first step; Involving and immersing stakeholders;* and *Provide rolling feedback.*

It is critical to pinpoint any mission drift - changes between what was recommended and what is being implemented - that could jeopardise the successful implementation of an insight.

Make a habit of developing the traits of the action mindset.

Next, we look at *Transformation* - how to embrace the new insight era.

20 TRANSFORMATION
How to be successful in the new customer insight era

The new customer insight paradigm calls for a *transformation* in the way that insight professionals operate. In this chapter we paint a picture of the role that customer insight professionals now need to play if they are to be successful in this new environment.

GUIDING PRINCIPLES

Principle One: Sensemaking skills will be at the heart of unearthing insights

Insight professionals will need to go beyond traditional data analysis skills to embrace a more holistic approach to making sense of today's complex often imperfect sources of data.

Principle Two: Futureproofing will be the primary role of the insight team

There will be a move away from insight just playing a more tactical role centred around minimising risk. Increasingly, the insight team will be at the leading edge of identifying and seizing business opportunities - ensuring the organisation manages disruption and change.

Principle Three: Detecting insights will draw on artificial intelligence combined with legacy insight skills

Specialists in artificial intelligence and other technical experts will be increasingly influential in unearthing insights. But the core skills of the customer insight professional will remain at the heart of the insight generation process. These centre on an in-depth understanding of the psychology of the consumer and expertise in measuring attitude (together with an appreciation of the ethics and legislation around data protection).

KEY ACTIONS

Action 1: Wide Angle Lens

Insight professionals will need to be the *wide angle lens* of the organisation. They see how everything connects together. They will be sensemakers with an acute sense of *what fits with what, what springs from what* and *what leads to what*.

They will be experts in seeing the overall *panorama* - how different insight stories fit together to give the big picture. This is the platform for identifying the implications for the successful management of change.

Action 2: Business Opportunity Leader

Customer insight professionals will be more focused on achieving business results than ever before. Specifically, they need to play the lead role in *futureproofing* the organisation. They need to be in the forefront of identifying and seizing business opportunities - helping to drive growth and manage disruption.

This will require insight professionals to combine the *telescopic* skills of seeing the big picture - being visionary - whilst also retaining the legacy *microscopic* skills of interpreting important detailed evidence.

Action 3: Whole Mind Power

Insight professionals will need the power of *Whole Mind* thinking in order to interpret customer behaviour. This ability to combine intuitive, creative right brain thinking with left brain grounded objectivity will become increasingly important.

Action 4: Agile Experimenter

Today's agile go-to-market process calls for *lean and agile thinking*. This is about being able to quickly identify and test the validity of the most critical factor underpinning an idea. The emphasis in unearthing insight is on setting up fast-to-implement, low-cost experiments that test critical assumptions early in the process - *test early and fail fast*.

It is about learning, adapting and improvising, and then overcoming. This approach allows norms and benchmarks to be built up about what is and is not working, and for these metrics to be a guide for decision-making - *predictive success modelling*.

The more agile go-to-market process changes the nature of the market research project management process. The original process was a linear one. But today, it is about being comfortable with beginning a journey with only a broad understanding of the overall direction of travel - with the confidence to course correct en route to the final destination.

Action 5: Creative Business Solutions Designer

Creativity will increasingly be at a premium in designing business solutions in today's highly competitive arena. This emphasis on creativity puts the focus on solving *problems* not just *puzzles*. With a puzzle there is always the comfort of a logical right/wrong, black/white answer. But with a problem, even when it is *solved*, there can remain a residue of uncertainty and ambiguity that needs to be negotiated and managed in arriving at a creative outcome.

This focus on creativity calls for customer insight professionals to provide what we might call *grounded creativity*. Creativity is a very disciplined business. Insights begin to emerge through the *disciplined eye* of looking at the data - but then become fully formed by applying some inspirational creativity.

This creativity reflects insight professionals' ability to look in from the *third corner* - from the customer perspective - to provide that creative *outside-in* perspective.

Action 6: Cognitive Collaboration

Increasingly, we will be relying on artificial intelligence to build our understanding of what drives customer behaviour. Consumer insights will, in part, be driven by the technology, but they will still need to be refined and nuanced by the insight team.

These are the professionals who can apply judgement and wisdom to an AI/ML generated solution by asking the critical *why* questions. This puts the focus on *Cognitive Collaboration* - humans and machines working together to arrive at the optimum solution.

FREQUENTLY ASKED QUESTIONS

Question One: Surely the new roles the customer insight professional must now play represent a total redefinition of the customer insight skillset?

> **Answer:** The good news is that this transformation - the new roles to be played - is grounded in the core legacy skills that customer insight professionals already possess. It is about having the confidence and belief to polish and refine these core skills and apply these in the new insight era.

Question Two: Is the new customer insight era, with the arrival of *black box* technology for generating insight, heralding the end of the traditional legacy skills of the customer insight professional?

> **Answer:** No, the ability of the customer insight professional to understand the psychology of the customer and ask appropriate *why* questions remains a powerful strength.

Question Three: Lots of different professionals, notably data scientists, are entering the customer insight space. Who do you think will be the winners and losers going forward in claiming the prize of being the insight experts?

> **Answer:** It is unhelpful to think of this as being about who wins and who loses. It becomes important for the insight professional to find ways of working in harmony with others generating insight, notably from AI/ML sources.

> However, it is important to reinforce the customer insight success story. So, it is beneficial to showcase your insight role. This is about *socialising your success* - deploying innovative communications techniques to demonstrate insight's role in setting the future direction of organisations.

Top Tip

Embrace the characteristics of the *growth,* as opposed to *fixed,* mindset. Develop the traits of flexibility and a willingness to learn, change and adapt. Find ways of *connecting* the best of what worked in the past with the new exciting opportunities available going forward. Build on core legacy skills: do not simply abandon the old and suddenly embrace stark new alternatives.

 Best Next Move

Look at each of the six roles where transformation will be required and score yourself on a scale of 1 to 10 (where 1 means little progress is being made and 10 means job done). Then develop a personal action plan to focus on areas where you need to make more rapid progress towards operating at a higher level on this dimension.

SUMMARY

The transformation of the customer insight skillset centres on the following six roles.

Be the *Wide Angle Lens.* Explain how everything connects to everything else.

Play a *Business Opportunity Leader* role. Focus on seizing opportunities to futureproof the organisation.

Operate with *Whole Mind* power. Be comfortable in creative and critical thinking modes.

Be an *Agile Experimenter.* Be a lean thinker and build the plane as you fly it.

Become a *Creative Business Solutions Designer*. Cultivate your creativity - this will be the big differentiator between success and failure.

Be in the vanguard of *Cognitive Collaboration.* Embrace AI/ML. Ask penetrating *why* questions to establish the veracity of AI generated insights.

In the next and final chapter, we look at the key *High Performance Habits* that customer insight professionals need to develop.

21 HIGH PERFORMANCE HABITS
How to build the High Performance Customer Insight Professional mindset

In this book we have provided ideas and techniques to develop the skills required to operate in the new customer insight era. However, to be a high performer, you need to turn these new enhanced skills into fundamental *habits* that you apply to everything you do. Aristotle said, *'We are what we repeatedly do... excellence is not an act but a habit'*. We now focus on seven fundamental success habits.

Habit One: Action

One of the key habits for being a successful customer insight professional is to *act* with intentionality to achieve your goals.

Tony Robbins, the success coach, claims that the path to success is to take massive determined action.

Bring your A-*Game* to every situation. Act with purpose and high energy to achieve excellence and deliver successful outcomes.

Habit Two: Focus

Highly successful people have the ability to *focus* on the top priority goals in a laser-like way, free from distraction.

Successful insight professional carve out the time to achieve their goals. They do not use a shortage of time as an excuse for not delivering *excellence* - they work at improving their productivity.

High performers will find ways of avoiding disruption and *energy and time robbers*. They will develop personal strategies for being effective and making a difference.

Habit Three: Clarity

High performing insight professionals see *clarity* of thinking as an ability that can be cultivated as a habit. They focus on designing simple but effective business solutions.

They find the process of *agonising* - wrestling with a problem in order to find the optimum solution - an enjoyable and rewarding experience.

High performers will develop the *forensic energy* required to be great *problem crystallisers* - making sure they are working on the right issue in an effective way. They will work on their problem solving skills. They enjoy *clear deep thinking* and value *problem cleaning*.

Habit Four: Creativity

Successful customer insight professionals make a habit of embracing techniques that will boost their *creativity* in their quest for innovative solutions.

Cultivating the creativity habit is based on the premise that being creative is *not* a gift that drifts down from the muse.

Clearly some people are more naturally creative than others, but practice and technique gets results. Everyone can follow processes and systems to improve their ability to think creatively.

Habit Five: Influence

The high performance insight professional recognises that it is legitimate to constructively *influence* evidence-based decisions - their mind is *admissible evidence.*

They recognise that cultivating the skill and confidence to be an influencer is a critical determinant of success.

Stakeholders are looking for insight professionals with presence, who instil confidence, are persuasive and express an informed point of view.

Habit Six: Courage

High performers will develop the mental strength - *courage* - to make sure any *doubters* do not sabotage their efforts to deliver world-class insight.

They will resist negative forces that are pulling them away from delivering the best possible outcome. They will not be deflected from their goals.

They are aware that there could be battles to be fought in the journey from being a data-provider to a trusted customer insight partner.

Habit Seven: Tenacity

The high performance insight professional recognises the importance of being *tenacious* - showing persistence in making things happen.

They recognise that they are in the business of achieving results, not just delivering presentations.

Successful insight professionals will make a habit of finding innovative ways of implementing their ideas.

The job is not done until you have turned your *Insights into Action!*

Notes

Part One: The Insight Sensemaker

1. A helpful guide to ensure you are working on the right problem is *Pig Wrestling - The Brilliantly Simple Way to Solve Any Problem and Create the Change You Need* (2019) Pete Lindsay & Mark Bawden

2. To help avoid default thinking see *The Moment of Clarity* (2014) Christian Madsbjerg & Mikkel B Rasmussen

3. A guide to core insight research legacy skills can be found in the ESOMAR *Market Research Handbook- Fifth edition* (2007)

4. For a review of the principles of data reduction see *A Primer in Data Reduction* (Reprinted 1994) ASC Ehrenberg

5. The importance of breaking down an analysis task into manageable elements is highlighted in *Six Thinking Hats* (1998) Edward de Bono

6. For an account of the power of combining left and right brain thinking in sensemaking can be found in *A Whole New Mind* (2008) Daniel H Pink

7. An introduction to the holistic approach to analysing data can be found in *The Art & Science of Interpreting Market Research Evidence* (2004) DVL Smith & JH Fletcher

Part Two: The Insight Story Builder

1. For the fundamentals behind System 1 and System 2 thinking see *Thinking, Fast and Slow* (2012) Daniel Kahneman

2. For a review of helpful business models around which to structure evidence see *The Business Models Handbook* (2019) Paul Hague

3. For ideas on the art of reinforcing the message with images see *The Visual Display of Quantitative Information* (2001) ER Tufte

4. To get behind the way great presenters think about the craft see *The Presentation Secrets of Steve Jobs: How to be Insanely Great in Front of Any Audience* (2010) Carmine Gallo

5. For tips on the art of presentation see *Presentation Zen - Simple Ideas on Presentation Design and Delivery* (2008) Garr Reynolds

6. For ideas on constructing compelling stories see *Presenting to win - The Art of Telling Your Story* (2009) Jerry Weissman

7. For further insights on constructing compelling narratives see *Slide:ology - The Art and Science of Creating Great Presentations* (2008) Nancy Duarte

Part Three: Insights into Action

1. For an account of the changing nature of the customer insight industry see *The Insights Revolution - Questioning Everything* (2018) Andrew Grenville

2. To learn more about agile ways of applying market insight evidence to marketing see *Where to Play - 3 Steps for Discovering Your Most Valuable Market Opportunities* (2017) Marc Gruber & Sharon Tal

3. For insights on stakeholders' expectations of internal customer insight teams see *How to Demonstrate the Value of Investing in Customer Insight* (2019) ESOMAR

4. For a discussion of the concepts of growth and fixed mindsets see *Mindset - Changing the way you think to fulfil your potential* (2006) Carol S Dweck

5. For a review of how to negotiate see *Getting to Yes: Negotiate an agreement without giving in* (2012) Roger Fisher, William Ury & Bruce Patton

6. For innovative ways of applying research evidence see *Change Ahead - How Research and Design are Transforming Business Strategy* (2015) Carola Verschoor

7. For an authoritative review of high performance habits see *High Performance Habits - How Extraordinary People Become That Way* (2007) Brendon Burchard

THE HIGH PERFORMANCE CUSTOMER INSIGHT
PROFESSIONAL CAPABILITY BUILDING PROGRAMMES

DVL Smith runs a range of Masterclasses, Action Workshops and Coaching programmes based on the ideas and techniques provided in this book.

Contact david.smith@dvlsmith.com

Made in the USA
San Bernardino, CA
13 November 2019